AMERICAN POLITICAL, ECONOMIC, AND SECURITY ISSUES SERIES

FOREIGN INVESTMENT IN U.S. SECURITIES

AMERICAN POLITICAL, ECONOMIC, AND SECURITY ISSUES SERIES

THE LAND AND MARITIME BOUNDARY DISPUTES OF THE AMERICAS
Rongxing Guo (Editor)
2009. ISBN: 978-1-60741-636-4

FOREIGN INVESTMENT IN U.S. SECURITIES
Declan J. Byrne (Editor)
2010. ISBN: 978-1-60876-084-8

AMERICAN POLITICAL, ECONOMIC, AND SECURITY ISSUES SERIES

FOREIGN INVESTMENT IN U.S. SECURITIES

DECLAN J. BYRNE
EDITOR

Nova Science Publishers, Inc.
New York

For permission to use material from this book please contact us:
Telephone 631-231-7269; Fax 631-231-8175
Web Site: http://www.novapublishers.com

LIBRARY OF CONGRESS CATALOGING-IN-PUBLICATION DATA

foreign investment in U.S. securities / editor, Declan J. Byrne.
p. cm.
Includes bibliographical references and index.
ISBN 978-1-60876-084-8 (softcover : alk. paper)
1. Investments, Foreign--United States. 2. Securities--United States. I. Byrne, Declan J.
HG4910.W39 2009
332.67'30973--dc22

2009032004

Published by Nova Science Publishers, Inc. ✝ New York

CONTENTS

PREFACE

Given its relatively low savings rate, the U.S. economy depends heavily on foreign capital inflows from countries with high savings rates (such as China) to help promote growth and to fund the federal budget deficit. Thus, foreign central banks and government-owned investment funds have played an important role financing the US current account deficit over the past several years. As the US economy has slowed relative to the rest of the world in late 2006, reducing the attractiveness of US financial of US financial assets to private investors abroad, the share of the US external deficit financed by foreign central banks increased substantially. This book will examine this increasing dependency of the U.S. economy on foreign investment.

Chapter 1 - Given its relatively low savings rate, the U.S. economy depends heavily on foreign capital inflows from countries with high savings rates (such as China) to help promote growth and to fund the federal budget deficit. China has intervened heavily in currency markets to limit the appreciation of its currency, especially against the dollar. As a result, China has become the world's largest and fastest growing holder of foreign exchange reserves (FER). China has invested a large share of its FER in U.S. securities, which, as of June 2008, totaled $1,205 billion, making China the 2nd largest foreign holder of U.S. securities (after Japan). These securities include long-term (LT) Treasury debt, LT U.S. agency debt, LT U.S. corporate debt, LT U.S. equities, and short-term debt.

U.S. Treasury securities are issued to finance the federal budget deficit. Of the public debt that is privately held, about half is held by foreigners. As of December 2008, China's Treasury securities holdings were $727 billion, accounting for 23.6% of total foreign ownership of U.S. Treasury securities, making it the largest foreign holder of U.S. Treasuries (replacing Japan in September 2008).

Chapter 2 – This is a testimony of Brad Setser, Senior Economist, Roubini Global Economics and Research Associate, before the House Budget Committee.

Chapter 3 - Foreign capital inflows are playing an important role in the U.S. economy by bridging the gap between domestic supplies of and demand for capital. In 2008, as the financial crisis and global economic downturn unfolded, foreign investors looked to U.S. Treasury securities as a "safe haven" investment, while they sharply reduced their net purchases of corporate stocks and bonds. Foreign investors now hold more than 50% of the publicly held and traded U.S. Treasury securities. The large foreign accumulation of U.S. securities has spurred some observers to arguethat this large foreign presence in U.S. financial markets increases the risk of a financial crisis, whether as a result of the uncoordinated actions of market participants or by a coordinated withdrawal from U.S. financial markets by foreign investors for economic or political reasons.

Chapter 4 - This report provides an overview of the role foreign investment plays in the U.S. economy and an assessment of possible actions a foreign investor or a group of foreign investors might choose to take to liquidate their investments in the United States. Concerns over the potential impact of disinvestment have grown as national governments have become more active investors and as uncertainty over the risks associated with securities backed by sub-prime mortgages has increased volatility in financial markets. Actions taken by foreign investors to liquidate their holdings could affect the U.S. economy in a number of ways due to the role foreign investment plays in the United States and due to the current mix of economic policies the United States has chosen. The impact of any such action on the economy would also depend on the overall condition and performance of the economy and the financial markets. If the economy were experiencing a strong rate of economic growth, the impact of a foreign withdrawal likely would be minimal, especially given the dynamic nature of credit markets. If a withdrawal occurred when the economy were not experiencing robust rate of growth or if credit financial markets were under duress, the withdrawal could have a stronger effect on the economy.

Chapter 5 - The international investment position of the United States is an annual measure of the assets Americans own abroad and the assets foreigners own in the United States. The net position, or the difference between the two, sometimes is referred to as a measure of U.S. international indebtedness. Although this designation is not strictly correct, the net international investment position does reveal the difference between the total assets Americans own abroad and total amount of assets foreigners own in the United States. These assets generate flows of capital into and out of the economy that have important implications for the value of the dollar in international exchange markets. Some Members of Congress and some in the public have expressed concerns about the U.S. net international investment position because of the role foreign investors are playing in U.S. capital markets and the potential for large outflows of income and services payments. Some observers also argue that the U.S. reliance on foreign capital inflows leaves the economy vulnerable to financial crises. This report will be updated as events warrant.

In: Foreign Investment In U.S. Securities
Editors: Declan J. Byrne
ISBN: 978-1-60876-084-8

Chapter 1

CHINA'S HOLDINGS OF U.S. SECURITIES: IMPLICATIONS FOR THE U.S.ECONOMY

Wayne M. Morrison and Marc Labonte

March 5, 2009

SUMMARY

Given its relatively low savings rate, the U.S. economy depends heavily on foreign capital inflows from countries with high savings rates (such as China) to help promote growth and to fund the federal budget deficit. China has intervened heavily in currency markets to limit the appreciation of its currency, especially against the dollar. As a result, China has become the world's largest and fastest growing holder of foreign exchange reserves (FER). China has invested a large share of its FER in U.S. securities, which, as of June 2008, totaled $1,205 billion, making China the 2nd largest foreign holder of U.S. securities (after Japan). These securities include long-term (LT) Treasury debt, LT U.S. agency debt, LT U.S. corporate debt, LT U.S. equities, and short-term debt.

U.S. Treasury securities are issued to finance the federal budget deficit. Of the public debt that is privately held, about half is held by foreigners. As of December 2008, China's Treasury securities holdings were $727 billion, accounting for 23.6% of total foreign ownership of U.S. Treasury securities, making it the largest foreign holder of U.S. Treasuries (replacing Japan in September 2008).

Some U.S. policymakers have expressed concern that China might try to use its large holdings of U.S. securities, including U.S. public debt, as leverage against U.S. policies it opposes. For example, in the past, some Chinese officials reportedly suggested that China could dump (or threaten to dump) a large share of its holdings to prevent the United States from imposing trade sanctions against China over its currency policy. Other Chinese officials reportedly stated that China should diversify its investments of its foreign exchange reserves away from dollar- denominated assets to those that offer higher rates of returns. The recent global financial crisis has heightened U.S. concerns that China might reduce its U.S. asset holdings.

A gradual decline in China's holdings of U.S. assets would not be expected to have a negative impact on the U.S. economy (since it could be matched by increased U.S. exports and a lower trade deficit). However, some economists contend that attempts by China to unload a large share of its U.S. securities holdings could have a significant negative impact on the U.S. economy (at least in the short run), especially if such a move sparked a sharp depreciation of the dollar in international markets and induced other foreign investors to sell off their U.S. holdings as well. In order to keep or attract that investment back, U.S. interest rates would rise, which would dampen U.S. economic growth, all else equal. Other economists counter that it would not be in China's economic interest to suddenly sell off its U.S. investment holdings. Doing so could lead to financial losses for the Chinese government, and any shocks to the U.S. economy caused by this action could ultimately hurt China's economy as well.

The issue of China's large holdings of U.S. securities is part of a larger debate among economists over how long the high U.S. reliance on foreign investment can be sustained, to what extent that reliance poses risks to the economy, and how to evaluate the costs associated with borrowing versus the benefits that would accrue to the economy from that practice. This report will be updated as events warrant.

Because of its low savings rate, the United States borrows to finance the federal budget deficit and its capital needs in order to enjoy healthy economic growth. It therefore depends on countries with high savings rates, such as China, to invest some of its capital in the United States.

China's central bank is a major purchaser of U.S. assets, largely because of its exchange rate policy. In order to limit the renminbi's (China's currency) appreciation against the dollar, China's central bank must purchase U.S. dollars.[1] This has led China to amass a huge level of foreign exchange reserves (FER); these totaled $1.95 trillion as of December 2008. Rather than hold dollars, which earn no interest, the Chinese central government has converted some level of its FER holdings into financial securities. Since foreign exchange holdings facilitate trade and prevent speculation against their currency, the central bank also holds securities from other foreign countries. The United States is a major destination of China's overseas investment. China is the second largest holder of U.S. securities, which include U.S. Treasury securities that are used to finance the federal budget deficit. Some U.S. policymakers have expressed concern that China's large holdings of U.S. securities may pose a risk to the U.S. economy should China stop purchasing those securities or attempt to divest itself of a large share of its holdings. In addition, China's FER are expected to continue to grow rapidly in the near future, potentially continuing (and possibly increasing) China's role as a major buyer of U.S. securities.

The recent financial crisis in the United States and the Administration's proposed plans to purchase troubled assets is expected to cost the government hundreds of billions of dollars, at least initially. This will require a substantial level of new government borrowing, some of which will likely be financed by foreign investors. China could be a major purchaser of new U.S. government debt.

This report examines the importance to the U.S. economy of China's investment in U.S. securities, as well as U.S. concerns over the possibility that China might unload a large share of those holdings, the likelihood that this would occur, and the potential implications such action could have for the U.S. economy. The report concludes that a large sell-off of Chinese Treasury securities holdings could negatively affect the U.S. economy, at least in the short-run. As a result, such a move could diminish U.S. demand for Chinese products and thus could lower China's economic growth as well. The issue of China's large holdings of U.S. securities is part of a broader question that has been raised by many economists: What are the implications of the heavy U.S. reliance on foreign investment to maintain healthy economic growth and to finance the budget deficit?[2]

CHINA'S FOREIGN EXCHANGE RESERVES

As indicated in **Table 1**, China's foreign exchange reserves have increased sharply in recent years, both in absolute terms and as a percent of gross domestic product (GDP). These rose from $216 billion in 2001 to $1,528 billion in 2007, to $1,946 billion as in 2008. China's reserves as a percent of

GDP grew from 15.3% in 2001 to 45% in 2008 - an unusually high level for a large economy.

Table 1. China's Foreign Exchange Reserves: 2001- 2008

Year	Billions of U.S. Dollars	As a % of Chinese GDP
2001	215.6	16.3
2002	291.1	20.0
2003	403.3	24.6
2004	609.9	31.6
2005	818.9	36.5
2006	1,068.5	40.2
2007	1,528.2	45.2
2008	1,946.0	45.0

Source: Global Insight and Chinese State Administration of Foreign Exchange.
Note: Year-end values.

Table 2. Top 5 Holders of Foreign Exchange Reserves and Changes to Holdings From 2006-2008

Country	Reserves (billions of U.S. dollars)			
	2006	2007	2008	Change in Reserves: 2006-2008
China	1,068.5	1,528.2	1,946.0	877.5
Japan	879.7	948.4	1,003.3	123.6
Russian Federation	295.3	386.2	406.2	110.9
	2006	2007	2008	Change in Reserves: 2006-2008
Taiwan	266.1	270.0	291.7	25.6
India	170.2	266.6	246.6	76.4

Sources: EIU Database, IMF International Financial Statistics, and Central Bank of the Republic of China (Taiwan).
Note: Ranked according to total holdings as of December 2008.

A listing of the world's top five holders of FER as of December 2008 is shown in **Table 2**. Not only was China by far the world's largest FER holder, its accumulation of additional reserves from 2006-2008 ($878 billion) was significantly larger than the combined FER increases of the other four major holders – Japan, Russia, Taiwan, and India.[3] According to the IMF, as of June 2008, China accounted for 26.2% of the world's FER.[4]

CHINA'S HOLDINGS OF U.S. SECURITIES[5]

China's central bank is a major purchaser of U.S. financial securities because of its exchange rate policy. In order to mitigate the renminbi's appreciation against the dollar, the central bank must purchase dollars. Rather than hold dollars, which earn no interest, the Chinese central government has converted some level of its foreign exchange holdings into financial securities. Since foreign exchange holdings facilitate trade and prevent speculation against their currency, the central bank also holds securities from other foreign countries.

There are no official estimates of what share of China's foreign reserves are held in dollar-denominated assets (assets that were bought with dollars and are cashed in dollars), but the Treasury Department conducts an annual survey of foreign portfolio holdings of U.S. securities by country, and reports data for the previous year as of the end of June.[6] The report does not distinguish between government and private holdings of U.S. securities. U.S. securities include long-term (LT) U.S. Treasury securities, LT U.S. government agency securities,[7] LT corporate securities (some of which are asset-backed), equities (such as stocks), and short-term debt.[8]

According to the latest Treasury survey of portfolio holdings of U.S. securities (issued in February 2009), China's total holdings as of June 2008 were $1,205 billion, which were $283 billion (or 31%) larger than June 2007 levels, and were nearly five times 2003 levels (see **Figure 1**).[9] These increases were significantly more than that of any other major foreign holder.[10]

As indicated in **Table 3**, China was the second largest foreign holder of U.S. securities, after Japan as of June 2008.[11] China may have become the largest foreign holder in late 2008 or early 2009. China's main holdings were in LT government agency securities and LT Treasury securities (see **Table 3**). This appears to indicate that the Chinese government has been pursuing a relatively low-risk investment strategy. In contrast, most of the United Kingdom's securities holdings were in corporate debt and equities. China's holdings of U.S. securities accounted for 11.7% of total foreign holdings of U.S. securities as of June 2008 (up from 9.4% as of June 2007).

Although the Chinese government does not make public the dollar composition of its foreign exchange holdings, many analysts estimate this level to be around 70%.[12] If this figure is correct, China's holdings of U.S. securities may have reached $1.36 trillion or higher as of December 2008.[13]

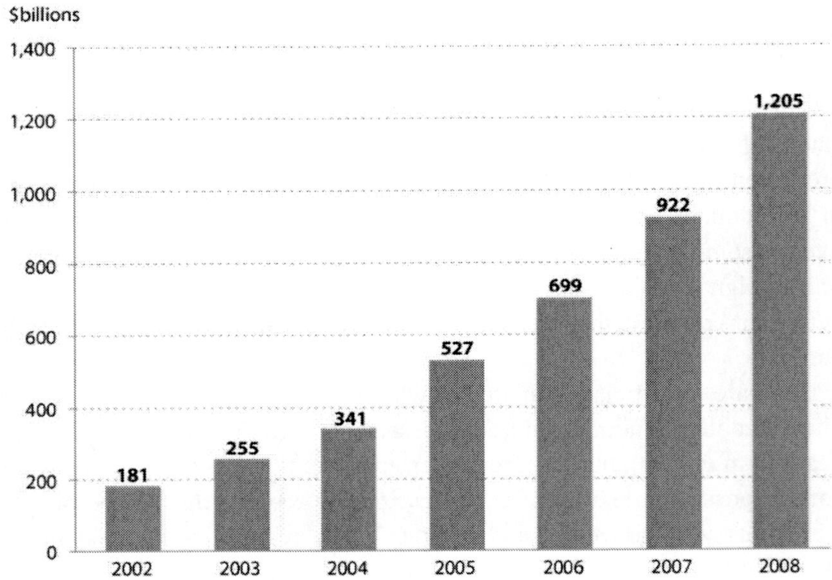

Source: U.S. Treasury Department, Preliminary Report On Foreign Holdings Of U.S. Securities At End-June 2008.

Figure 1. China's Holdings of U.S. Securities: June 2002-June 2008 $billions

It is not clear to what extent China's investments have gone into U.S. sub-prime mortgage securities, but they are likely to be small relative to their total investments. As seen in **Table 3**, China has invested $527 billion in long-term agency securities, most—but not all—of which is likely to be debt issued by Fannie Mae and Freddie Mac. *The South China Morning Post* (September 25, 2008) estimated that Chinese banks held $9.8 billion in U.S. sub-prime loans at the end of 2007 and $25 billion in Fannie Mae and Freddie Mac securities as of June 30, 2008. Whatever risk China faced from its holdings of Freddie Mac and Fannie Mae mortgage-backed securities was greatly reduced in September 2008 when these two institutions were placed in conservatorship by the Federal Government and thus have government backing. The Bank of China (one of China's largest state-owned commercial banks) reportedly had the largest exposures to U.S. sub-prime mortgage-backed securities among any banks in Asia when the financial crisis began. However, it reported that holdings of such securities as a share of its total investment securities portfolio were reduced from 3.5% in March 2008 to 1.4% in October 2008.[14]

U.S. data indicate Chinese holdings of U.S. agency debt from June 2007 to June 2008 increased by $151 billion (all of this increase was in asset-backed securities) and accounted for over half of China's increased holdings of total U.S. securities in 2008. China's new purchases of new agency debt were bigger than that of any other foreign country over this one year period. China is by far the largest foreign owner of U.S. agency debt, accounting for 36% of total foreign holdings (up from 29% as of June 2007). The second biggest category of new U.S. securities holdings in 2008 was in equities, which increased by $71 billion.

It is not yet clear how the U.S. sub-prime and financial crisis and ensuing global financial crisis has affected China's purchases of U.S. securities, especially since the extent of these crises became more apparent after June 2008. [1] For example, in September 2008, Fannie Mae and Freddie Mac were placed in conservatorship by the Federal Government. Press reports indicate that China, which is believed to hold a large amount of Freddie Mac and Fannie Mae securities, was greatly concerned over the financial safety of its holdings when it became clear in July 2008 that both institutions were in serious financial trouble. The U.S. government takeover of Freddie Mac and Fannie Mae provided explicit U.S. government backing to these securities.

China's Ownership of U.S. Treasury Securities[15]

U.S. Treasury securities are the main vehicle the U.S. government uses to finance the federal debt, which totaled $10.0 trillion at the end of September 2008. Of this amount, 47% was held by U.S. government trust funds and 53% was privately held. Of the total level of privately-held U.S. Treasury securities ($5.3 trillion), foreigners owned 54% of the total ($2.9 trillion).[16] China's holdings of U.S. Treasury securities holdings (as of September 2008) accounted for 11.0% of total private holdings (including foreign governments and citizens) of U.S. Treasury securities and 5.9% of total U.S. public debt securities (combined public and private).[17]

Table 3.Top Three Foreign Holders of U.S. Securities as of June 2008 ($ billions)

Type of Security	Total	LT Treasury	LT Government Agency	LT Corporate	Equities	Short Term
Japan	1,250	568	270	148	199	66
China	**1,2051**	**522**	**527**	**26**	**100**	**30**
United Kingdom	864	45	26	394	376	24
World Total	10,324	2,210	1,464	2,820	2,969	861
Change in China's Holdings over June 2007	**283**	**55**	**151**	**-2**	**71**	**7**
China's Holdings as a Percent of World Total (%)	**11.7**	**23.6**	**36.0**	**0.9**	**3.4**	**3.5**

Source: U.S. Treasury Department, Preliminary *Report on Foreign Portfolio Holdings of U.S. Securities as of June* 30, 2008, February 2009.

Note: LT securities are those with no stated maturity date (such as equities) or with an original term to maturity date of more than one year. Short term securities have a maturity period of less than one year.

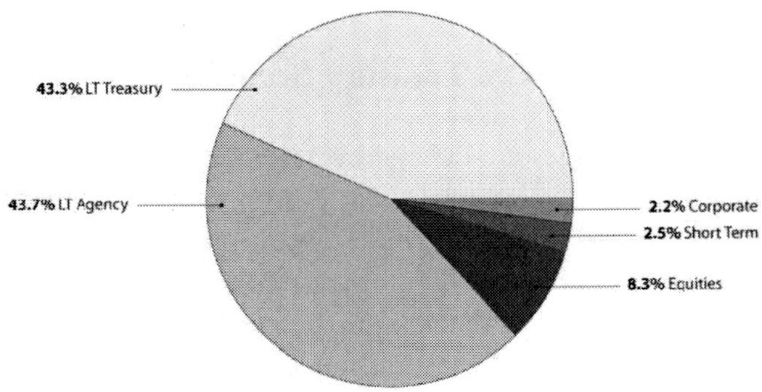

Source: Department of Treasury.

Note: LT stands for long-term debt.

Figure 2. Composition of China's Holdings of U.S. Securities as of June 2008

Table 4. China's Holdings of U.S.Treasury Securities: 2002-2008Year-End
$billions and as a percent of total foreign holdings

	2002	2003	2004	2005	2006	2007	2008
China's Holdings ($billions)	118.4	159.0	222.9	310.0	396.9	477.6	727.4
Holdings as a % of Total Forei-gn Holdings	9.6%	10.4%	12.1%	15.2%	18.9%	20.3%	23.6%

Source: U.S. Treasury Department.

Table 5. Major Foreign Holders of U.S.Treasury Securities: December 2007 and December 2008 ($ billions)

	Dec 2007	Dec 2008	Dec 2007-Dec 2008 Change in the Value of its Holdings	Holdings as a Share of Total Foreign Holdings as of Dec 2008 (%)
China	477.6	727.4	249.8	23.6
Japan	579.9	626.0	46.1	20.3
Caribbean Banking Centers	117.4	197.5	80.1	6.4
Oil Exporters[a]	137.9	186.2	48.3	6.3
United Kingdom	157.9	130.9	-27.0	4.3
Total Foreign Holdings	2,351.1	3,076.9	725.8	100.0

Source: Department of Treasury, *Major Foreign Holders of Treasury Securities Holdings*, February 27, 2008.

a. Oil exporters include Ecuador, Venezuela, Indonesia, Bahrain, Iran, Iraq, Kuwait, Oman, Qatar, Saudi Arabia, the United Arab Emirates, Algeria, Gabon, Libya, and Nigeria.

Note: *Data are based on surveys which are done annually or biannually. A new survey may often significantly revise data of a previous survey. Thus, time series data should be viewed with caution.

Table 5 lists the top five major foreign holders of U.S. Treasury securities as of December 2008. China was the largest holder of U.S. Treasury Securities (overtaking Japan in September 2008) at $724 billion; it was the 7th largest holder in December 1997.[18] Over the past few years, China has become a major purchaser of Treasury securities. From December 2002 to December 2008, China's share of total foreign holdings of U.S. Treasury securities rose from 9.6% to 23.6%. From December 2007 to December 2008, China's holdings increased by $250 billion (or 52.3%), by far the largest dollar increase of any country. China accounted for 34.4% of net new holdings of U.S. Treasury securities in 2008. In comparison, Japan's holdings rose by $46.1 billion. China's purchases of U.S. Treasury securities were relatively large in September and October 2008, at $44.5 billion and $65.9 billion, respectively. This may in part reflect a movement by China (and other foreign investors) away from purchases of U.S. agency asset-backed securities (such those issued by Fannie Mae and Freddie Mac) to more "safe" U.S. Treasury securities (especially short- term securities).

U.S. Concerns Over China's Large Holdings of U.S. Securities

Some U.S. policymakers have expressed concern over China's large holdings of U.S. securities, including Treasury securities, contending that China could use it as a political tool against the United States. To illustrate, an August 7, 2007 article in the *Telegraph* (an online British newspaper) cited interviews with officials from two leading Chinese government think tanks who reportedly stated that China had the power to make the dollar collapse (if it chose to do so) by liquidating large portions of its U.S. Treasury securities holdings if the United States imposed trade sanctions to force a renminbi revaluation, and that the threat to do so could be used as a "bargaining chip."[19] The article prompted concern among many U.S. policymakers, including Senator Chuck Grassley, who, in an August 9, 2007 letter to the Chinese ambassador to the United States (Zhou Wenzhong), called the comments "dangerous" and a factor in why the United States "is right to be concerned with China's currency practices." The letter asked the Chinese government to confirm that "the comments do not reflect the official position of the Chinese government."[20] In response, the Chinese ambassador wrote to Senator Grassley on August 13, 2007, that "China does not have a plan to drastically adjust the structure of its foreign reserves."[21] In addition, China's *Xinhua News Agency* on August 13, 2007, quoted an unnamed official at the People's Bank of China as stating that "dollar-denominated assets, including U.S.

government securities, are an important component in China's foreign exchange reserve investment portfolio," and that China was "a responsible investor."

Numerous reports have appeared in the media citing various Chinese officials who, in the past, have claimed or hinted at government plans to reduce its holdings of U.S. Treasury securities for economic reasons. For example, on September 29, 2007, the Chinese government officially launched the state-owned *China Investment Corporation*, which Chinese officials state was created to better manage its foreign exchange reserves. It reportedly will initially manage over $200 billion of China's reserves, making it one of the world's largest sovereign wealth funds. Some contend the creation of this entity could signal Chinese plans to diversify away from relatively low-yielding assets, such as Treasury securities, and perhaps dollar-denominated assets in general.[22] On November 7, 2007, Cheng Siwei, the vice chairman of the Chinese National People's Congress, reportedly made remarks that the Chinese government "will favor stronger currencies over weaker ones, and will readjust accordingly." The media claimed that his remarks were a major factor in sparking a sharp decline of the dollar against the euro in international currency markets that day.[23] However, on November 14, 2007, Yi Gang, assistant governor of the People's Bank of China, was quoted as saying that "the U.S. dollar is the main currency in our reserves and that policy remains very firm," and said that statements by other officials to the contrary were "opinions."[24]

Some U.S. policymakers have recently raised concerns that China, for economic reasons (such as concerns over the safety of its current holdings of U.S. securities), might seek to liquidate such assets or significantly cut back on purchases of new securities. These fears have been heightened as a result of the U.S. sub-prime mortgage crisis and the subsequent global financial crisis.[25] At a press conference during her visit to China on February 21, 2009, Secretary of State Hillary Rodham Clinton brought up this issue, stating that she appreciated "greatly the Chinese government's continuing confidence in the United States treasuries."

WHAT IF CHINA REDUCES ITS HOLDINGS OF U.S. SECURITIES?[26]

As the previous data illustrate, China has accumulated large holdings of U.S. assets in recent years. These accumulations are the result of U.S. borrowing to finance its large trade deficit with China (the gap between U.S. exports and Chinese imports). All else equal, Chinese government purchases of U.S. assets increases the demand for U.S. assets, which reduces U.S. interest rates.

If China attempted to reduce its holdings of U.S. securities, they would be sold to other investors (foreign and domestic), who would presumably require higher interest rates than those prevailing today to be enticed to buy them. One analyst estimates that a Chinese move away from long-term U.S. securities could raise interest rates by as much as 50 basis points.[27] Higher interest rates would cause a decline in investment spending and other interest-sensitive spending. All else equal, the reduction in Chinese Treasury holdings would cause the overall foreign demand for U.S. assets to fall, and this would cause the dollar to depreciate. If the value of the dollar depreciated, the trade deficit would decline, as the price of U.S. exports fell abroad and the price of imports rose in the United States.[28] The magnitude of these effects would depend on how many U.S. securities China sold; modest reductions would have negligible effects on the economy given the vastness of U.S. financial markets.

Since China held $1,205 billion of U.S. government assets as of June 2008 (and possibly $1.4 trillion at the end of 2008), any reduction in its U.S. holdings could potentially be large. If there were a large reduction in its holdings, the effect on the U.S. economy would still depend on whether the reduction were gradual or sudden. It should be emphasized that economic theory suggests that a *slow decline* in the trade deficit and dollar would not be troublesome for the overall economy. In fact, a slow decline could even have an expansionary effect on the economy, if the decrease in the trade deficit had a more stimulative effect on aggregate demand in the short run than the decrease in investment and other interest-sensitive spending resulting from higher interest rates. Historical experience seems to bear this out—the dollar declined by about 40% in real terms and the trade deficit declined continually in the late 1980s, from 2.8% of GDP in 1986 to nearly zero during the early 1990s. Yet economic growth was strong throughout the late 1980s.

A potentially serious short-term problem would emerge if China decided to *suddenly* reduce their liquid U.S. financial assets significantly. The effect could be compounded if this action triggered a more general financial reaction (or panic), in which all foreigners responded by reducing their holdings of U.S. assets. The initial effect could be a sudden and large depreciation in the value of the dollar, as the supply of dollars on the foreign exchange market increased, and a sudden and large increase in U.S. interest rates, as an important funding source for investment and the budget deficit was withdrawn from the financial markets. The dollar depreciation would not cause a recession since it would ultimately lead to a trade surplus (or smaller deficit), which expands aggregate demand.[29] (Empirical evidence suggests that the full effects of a change in the exchange rate on traded goods takes time, so the dollar may have to "overshoot" its eventual depreciation level in order to achieve a significant adjustment in trade flows in the short run.)[30] However, a sudden increase in interest rates could swamp the trade effects and cause (or worsen) a recession. Large increases in interest rates could cause problems for the U.S. economy, as these increases reduce the market value of debt securities, cause prices on the stock market to fall, undermine efficient financial intermediation, and jeopardize the solvency of various debtors and creditors. Resources may not be able to shift quickly enough from interest-sensitive sectors to export sectors to make this transition fluid. The Federal Reserve could mitigate the interest rate spike by reducing short-term interest rates, although this reduction would influence long-term rates only indirectly, and could worsen the dollar depreciation and increase inflation.

The likelihood that China would suddenly reduce its holdings of U.S. securities is questionable because it is doubtful that doing so would be in China's economic interests. First, a large sell-off of China's U.S. holdings could diminish the value of these securities in international markets, which would lead to large losses on the sale, and would, in turn, decrease the value of China's remaining dollar-denominated assets.[31] This would also occur if the value of the dollar were greatly diminished in international currency markets due to China's sell-off [32] Second, such a move would diminish U.S. demand for Chinese imports, either through a rise in the value of the renminbi against the dollar or a reduction in U.S. economic growth (especially if other foreign investors sold their U.S. asset holdings, and the United States was forced to raise interest rates in response).[33] According to some estimates, nearly one quarter of Chinese exports went to the United States in 2008. A sharp reduction of U.S. imports from China could have a significant impact on China's economy, which heavily depends on exports for its economic growth (and is viewed by the government as a vital source of political stability).[34] Finally, any major action by the Chinese government that destabilized (or further destabilized) the U.S. economy (whether deliberate or not) could provoke "protectionist" sentiment in the United States against China.

CONCLUDING OBSERVATIONS

Many economists argue that concerns over China's holdings of U.S. securities represent part of a broader problem for the U.S. economy, namely its dependence on foreign saving to finance its investment needs and federal budget deficits.[35] The large U.S. current account deficit (the manifestation of the high U.S. saving/investment gap) cannot be sustained indefinitely because the U.S. net foreign debt cannot rise faster than GDP indefmitely.[36] Some economists argue that at some point foreign investors may view the growing level of U.S. foreign debt as unsustainable or more risky, or they may no longer view U.S. securities as offering the best return on their investment, and shift investment funds away from U.S. assets, thus forcing U.S. interest rates to rise to attract needed foreign capital. This would result in higher interest rates and lower investment rates, all else equal, which would reduce long-term growth.[37] Other economists contend that, although the low U.S. savings rate is a problem, the U.S. current account deficit and high levels of foreign capital flows to the United States are also reflections of the strength of the U.S. economy and its attractiveness as a destination for foreign investment, and therefore discount the likelihood that foreign investors will suddenly shift their capital elsewhere.[38]

The United States continues to press China to make its currency policy more flexible so that the renminbi will appreciate more significantly against the dollar and to adopt policies that promote domestic consumption as a major source of China's economic growth (as opposed to export and fixed investment-led growth that has resulted from China's currency policy).[39] This is viewed as a major step towards reducing global trade imbalances, including the large U.S.-China trade imbalance. However, in order for that to occur, the United States must also boost its level of savings in the long run. If China consumed more and saved less, it would have less capital to invest overseas, including in the United States. Thus, if the United States did not reduce its dependence on foreign savings for its investment needs, and China reduced its U.S. investments, the United States would need to obtain investment from other countries, and the overall U.S. current account balance would likely remain relatively unchanged.

Some U.S. policymakers have expressed hope that China will increase its U.S. debt holdings in order to help the Federal government pay for its financial rescue plan and future stimulus packages.[40] But others have expressed concern that becoming more reliant on Chinese purchases of U.S. debt would increase China's political leverage over the United States and may make it more difficult for the United States to induce China to appreciate its currency more quickly and to make other needed reforms to its economy. Some analysts contend that economic factors in China, such as decreased exports and foreign direct investment flows to China, may sharply limit its accumulation of additional foreign exchange reserves, which in turn could slow or halt China's purchases of U.S. securities.

ENDNOTES

[1] China's accumulation of foreign exchange reserves has also occurred because of large annual current account trade surpluses, high levels of foreign direct investment in China, and inflows of "hot money" from overseas investors who anticipate that the Chinese government will appreciate the renminbi in the near future. For additional information, see CRS Report RL32165, *China's Currency: Economic Issues and Options for U.S. Trade Policy*, by Wayne M. Morrison and Marc Labonte.

[2] For a discussion of the implications of a possible global sell-off of U.S. securities, see CRS Report RL34319, *Foreign Ownership of U.S. Financial Assets: Implications of a Withdrawal*, by James K. Jackson.

[3] China overtook Japan in 2006 to become the world's largest holder of FER.

[4] Total reserves for all countries in June 2008 were estimated at $6,894.1 billion. Worldwide, 41% of reserves were held in dollar-denominated assets.

[5] For additional information on foreign ownership of U.S. securities, see CRS Report RL32462, *Foreign Investment in U.S. Securities*, by James K. Jackson.

[6] Note, Treasury's annual survey does not include data on foreign direct investment (FDI) in the United States, which measures foreign ownership or investment in U.S. businesses. China's total FDI in the U.S. at the end of 2007 was $1.1 billion (on a historical cost basis), according the U.S. Bureau of Economic Analysis. Since these types of assets cannot be liquidated rapidly, they are not included in this report.

[7] Agency securities include both federal agencies and government-sponsored enterprises created by Congress (e.g., Fannie Mae and Freddie Mac) to provide credit to key sectors of the economy. Some of these securities are backed by assets (such as home mortgages).

[8] LT securities are those with no stated maturity date (such as equities) or with an original term to maturity date of more than one year. Short-term debt includes U.S. Treasury securities, agency securities, and corporate securities with a maturity date of less than one year.

[9] Data on China's holdings of U.S. securities exclude holdings by Hong Kong (which totaled $147 billion as of June 20080 and Macao. These entities, though part of China, are reported separately by Treasury.

[10] In comparison, Japan's holdings grew by only $53 billion.

[11] According to the Treasury Department, data on foreign holdings of U.S. securities should be treated with caution, due to the difficulty in obtaining accurate information on the *actual* foreign owners of U.S. securities. For example, chains of foreign financial intermediaries may be involved in the custody or management of these securities.

[12] See testimony of Brad Setser, Senior Economist, Roubini Global Economics and Research Associate, Global Economic Governance Programme, University College, Oxford, before the House Budget Committee, *Foreign Holdings of U.S. Debt: Is our Economy Vulnerable?*, June 26, 2007, p. 11. In addition, the *People's Daily Online* (August 28, 2006) estimated China's dollar holdings to total FER at 70%.

[13] Some analysts contend that the Chinese government undercounts the total level of its foreign exchange reserves and thus, its holdings of U.S. securities could be even higher.

[14] The Bank of China either reduced its holdings or wrote off the losses.

[15] For a general discussion of foreign ownership of U.S. debt, see CRS Report RS22331, *Foreign Holdings of Federal Debt*, by Justin Murray and Marc Labonte.

[16] U.S. Treasury Department, Financial Management Service, *Ownership of Federal Securities*, available at http://www.fms.treas.gov/bulletin/index.html.

[17] Although yields on U.S. Treasury securities are relatively low compared to other types of investment, they are also considered to be relatively low in risk. Thus they are viewed by many central banks to be a safe investment for their FER.

[18] Treasury constantly revises its estimates of foreign holdings of U.S. securities. On February 27, 2009, it made substantial revisions to its previously released monthly data for 2008 (which was issued on February 17, 2009). The new data raised estimates for China's holdings of U.S. Treasury securities in December 2008 from $696 billion (old estimate) to $727 billion. However, Treasury does not revise its data from previous years. Thus, comparisons of historical Treasury data should be viewed with caution.

[19] The Telegraph, *China Threatens 'Nuclear Option' of Dollar Sales*, August 7, 2007.

[20] See text of letter at http://grassley.senate.gov/public/.

[21] Letter reprinted in *Inside U.S. Trade*, August 13, 2007.

[22] Others are concerned that China will attempt to use the fund to purchase major U.S. companies. See the New Yorker, *Sovereign Wealth World*, November 26, 2007. According to the article, "were China's fund so inclined, it could buy Ford, G.M., Volkswagen, and Honda, and still have a little money left over for ice cream."

[23] *Bloomberg News*, November 8, 2007.

[24] *China Daily*, November 15, 2007.

[25] See CRS Report RL34742, *The Global Financial and Economic Crisis: Analysis and Policy Implications*, coordinated by Dick K. Nanto.

[26] From the perspective of the macroeconomic effects on U.S. investment, interest rates, and so on, it does not matter what type of U.S. security is purchased when foreign capital flows to the United States. Thus, Chinese purchases of all types of U.S. securities (not just Treasury securities) should be considered when attempting to understand the impact China's investment decisions have on the U.S. economy.

[27] Testimony of Brad Setser before the House Budget Committee, *Foreign Holdings of U.S. Debt: Is our Economy Vulnerable?*, June 26, 2007. Brad Setser is Senior Economist, Roubini Global Economics, and Research Associate, Global Economic Governance Programme, University College, Oxford. Setser does not detail how much U.S. debt he assumes China would sell to reach his estimate.

[28] The extent that the dollar declined and U.S. interest rates rose would depend on how willing other foreigners were to supplant China's reduction in capital inflows. A greater willingness would lead to less dollar depreciation and less of an increase in interest rates, and vice versa.

[29] A sharp decline in the value of the dollar would also reduce living standards, all else equal, because it would raise the price of imports to households. This effect, which is referred to as a decline in the terms of trade, would not be recorded directly in GDP, however.

[30] Since the decline in the dollar would raise import prices, this could temporarily increase inflationary pressures. The effect would likely be modest, however, since imports are small as a share of GDP and import prices would only gradually rise in response to the fall in the dollar.

[31] Since there are many other holders of U.S. assets, it is possible that if China believed a decline in asset values was imminent, it could minimize its losses by dumping its U.S. assets first, however.

[32] Selling off U.S. dollar assets could cause the renminbi to appreciate against the dollar, which would lower the value of remaining U.S. assets since the assets are dollar-denominated.

[33] In addition, if a "dollar collapse" occurred, U.S. imports from other major trade partners would decline, which could slow their economies. This in turn could weaken their demand for Chinese products.

[34] Although a falling dollar may harm China's short-term growth via reduced Chinese exports (and export sector- related employment), it would also improve China's terms of trade with the United States, raising China's overall consumption since it could now spend less to acquire the same amount of American goods (which would also create jobs in other sectors of the economy because of increased consumer purchasing power).

[35] Nations (such as the United States) that fail to save enough to meet their investment needs must obtain savings from other countries with high savings rates (such as China) By obtaining resources from foreign investors for its investment needs, the United States is able to enjoy a higher rate of consumption than it would if investment were funded by domestic savings alone. The inflow of foreign capital to the United States is equivalent to the United States borrowing from the rest of the world. The only way the United States can borrow from the rest of the world is by importing more than it exports, which produces a trade (and current account) deficit.

[36] The current account deficit rose from $389.4 billion in 2002 to $811.5 billion in 2006, and as a percent of GDP, it increased from 4.4% to 6.1%, respectively. The Economist Intelligence Unit estimates that the current account deficit as a percent of GDP 5.3% in 2007 and to 4.8% in 2008.

[37] See CRS Report RL33186, Is *the U.S. Current Account Deficit Sustainable?,* by Marc Labonte.

[38] See Council of Economic Advisors, Economic Report of the President, *The U.S. Capital Surplus*, February 2006, p. 144.

[39] In November, the Chinese government announced it would implement a two-year $586 billion stimulus package, mainly dedicated to infrastructure projects.

[40] See CRS Report RS22984, *China and the Global Financial Crisis: Implications for the United States*, by Wayne M. Morrison.

In: Foreign Investment In U.S. Securities
Editors: Declan J. Byrne
ISBN: 978-1-60876-084-8

Chapter 2

"FOREIGN HOLDINGS OF US DEBT: IS OUR ECONOMY VULNERABLE?"

Brad Setser

I want to thank the members of the committee for inviting me to testify. It is a particular honor to participate in such a distinguished panel.

At the end of 2006, foreigners held an estimated $10 trillion in US debt – roughly $5 trillion in long-term debt securities and $5 in short-term securities and cross-border bank claims. Roughly $800 billion of the $5 trillion in long-term claims were held by China's government (counting some securities held by China's state commercial banks) more than the perhaps $700 billion in long-term US debt securities held by Japan's government.[1] By the end of 2007, total foreign holdings of US debt will rise to around $12 trillion, total foreign holdings of long-term debt securities will be close to $6 trillion, and long-term debt held by China's government likely will rise to around $1.1 trillion.

I mention China specifically because the strong recent rise in China's current account surplus, along with ongoing private capital inflows into China, has made China's government the largest single source of (net) financing for the US current account deficit. China's foreign exchange reserves – counting the reserves likely to be shifted to a new investment agency – are set to rise by between $450 and $500 billion in 2007, with between $300 and $350 billion of that increase flowing into US assets (Chart 1). China's foreign assets are growing so rapidly that it could buy a company the size of Unocal every month – and still have enough money left over to buy all the Treasury bonds that the US needs to sell to finance its budget deficit. Right now, China's government is the largest single buyer of US Treasury and US "Agency" bonds, the largest potential source of demand for many other dollar-denominated financial assets and – given that it must sell a fraction of the dollars it accumulates intervening in the foreign exchange market to keep the dollar share of its reserves from rising – also the largest actor in the foreign exchange market.

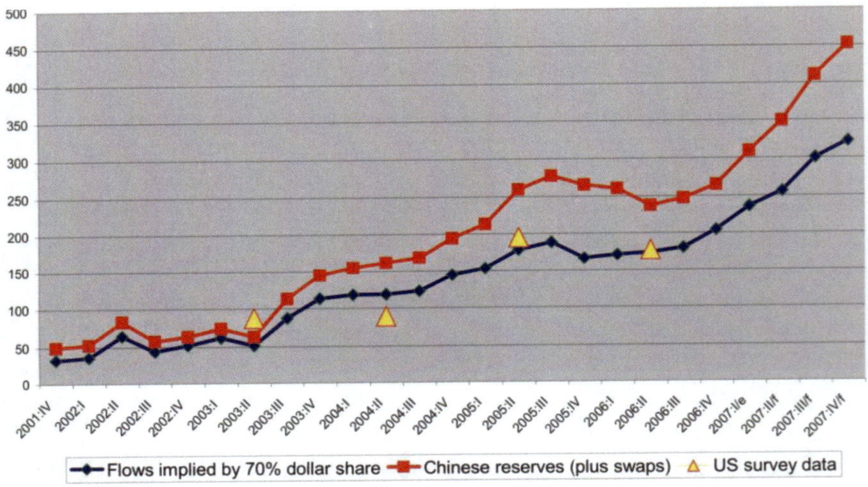

Chart 1. Chinese purchases of US dollar-denominated debt debt $ billion; rolling four quarter sums; 2007 forecast

Financial integration implies rising foreign holdings of US assets and rising US holdings of foreign assets. But so long as the US is running a large external deficit, foreign holdings of US assets will need to rise faster than US holdings of foreign assets. The large US current account deficit – roughly $800b in 2006 – has been financed primarily by placing debt, and specifically long-term debt securities, with foreign investors. US direct investment abroad, along with US purchases of foreign equities, recently have exceeded foreign direct investment in the US and foreign purchases of US equities.

My testimony will emphasize three points:

To date, the United States' large trade deficit has not resulted to a significant deterioration in the United States' net international investment position (US liabilities to the world net of US holdings of foreign assets) or to a deficit in the income balance (the gap between the interest and dividends the United States receives on its investments abroad and the interest and dividends the United States pays to foreigners). Going forward, that is likely to change. The United States should not expect foreigners – including foreign governments – to finance the United States on as generous terms as the US has enjoyed over the past few years.

Foreign central banks and government-owned investment funds have played an important role financing the US current account deficit over the past several years. As the US economy has slowed relative to the rest of the world in late 2006, reducing the attractiveness of US financial assets to private investors abroad, the share of the US external deficit financed by foreign central banks increased substantially.

Official financial flows have generally been stabilizing rather than destabilizing; foreign central banks have bought dollar-denominated assets, financing the US deficit, when private investors haven't wanted to. Bringing the US deficit down in a gradual, orderly way will require ongoing central bank financing. However, the United States ongoing dependence on inflows from foreign central banks still poses substantial risks. The US should worry both about the possibility that foreign central banks will provide the US with too little financing, forcing rapid and disruptive adjustment, and the possibility that foreign central banks will provide the US with so much financing that a necessary adjustment is deferred.

One theme will run throughout my testimony: the United States has a strong interest in a process of gradual adjustment that reduces the United States' need to borrow from the rest of the world to finance domestic investment. The absence of any adjustment is undesirable: it implies that foreigners will continue to finance a very large share of all US domestic investment and a large buildup of the United States' foreign debt. Too rapid adjustment is also undesirable. A sharp fall in foreign financing of the US would lead the dollar to fall, stimulating US exports, but it would also push up US interest rates, leading other parts of the economy to slow. Gradual adjustment – say 1% of GDP a year — would facilitate the shift of resource from sectors of the economy that have benefited from the low interest rates associated with large (net) inflow of foreign savings to the US toward sectors that would benefit from a weaker dollar. Gradual adjustment also provides foreign governments time to take steps to stimulate domestic demand and wean their economies off export-led growth.

THE ONGOING INCREASE IN FOREIGN HOLDINGS OF US DEBT IS UNLIKELY TO CONTINUE ON SUCH GENEROUS TERMS

The United States' current account deficit topped \$800b — roughly 6% of US GDP – in 2006. Its 2007 deficit is likely to be comparable in size. As the US economy emerges from its recent growth slump, the US current account deficit is likely to resume its increase in the absence of a fall in oil prices or large additional falls in the dollar.

Right now, the current account surpluses that offset the US deficit are overwhelmingly found in East Asia and the world's oil-exporting economies. Should oil prices stabilize, rising domestic spending and investment in the oil-exporting economies should reduce their current account surplus. However, East Asia's surplus looks set to continue its rise. China's current account surplus was \$250b (a bit under 10% of China's GDP) in 2006.

Its 2007 surplus is expected to rise to \$350-400b – an unprecedented sum. Japan's current account surplus is also rising, in part because of rising interest income from Japan's large holdings of foreign debt. So long as East Asia's surplus continues to rise, global adjustment will be difficult. Surpluses in one region have to be offset by deficits elsewhere.

A current account deficit indicates that a country saves less than it invests; a surplus indicates a surplus of savings over investment. The US consequently must finance its savings shortfall either by placing debt with investors in the rest of the world, attracting large (net) inflows into its equity market or attracting large net inflows of foreign direct investment. New foreign equity investments in the US – whether direct investment or the purchase of foreign stocks– have been more than offset by new US equity investments abroad. Inflows into the US banking system have generally been offset by outflows from the US banking system. By contrast, foreign purchases of US debt securities have exceeded US purchases of foreign debt, providing the large net inflows needed to cover the United States current account deficit.

As a result, the US net debt position – the gap between what the US has borrowed from the world and what the US has lent to the world -- has deteriorated dramatically over the past six years. Since the end of 2000, total foreign holdings of US debt have increased from $4.3 trillion to close to $10.0 trillion while US lending to the rest of the world has increased from $2.9 trillion to an estimated $4.6 trillion. Net US external debt consequently has increased from $1.5 trillion at the end of 2000 to about $5.4 trillion at the end of 2006 – the $4 trillion increase is in line with the cumulative $3.6 trillion US current account deficit over this time frame.

However, the overall US net international investment position – the difference between all US assets abroad and all US liabilities to the world — hasn't deteriorated at the same pace. The dollar value of US equity investment abroad has increased far more rapidly that the dollar value of foreign equity investment in the US. The dollar value of US equity investment abroad increased from $4.5 trillion in 2000 to $9.1 trillion in 2006, while the dollar value of foreign equity investment in the US increased from $4.3 trillion to an estimated $5.9 trillion. The United States' net equity position consequently shifted from rough balance to a $3 trillion surplus (Chart 2).

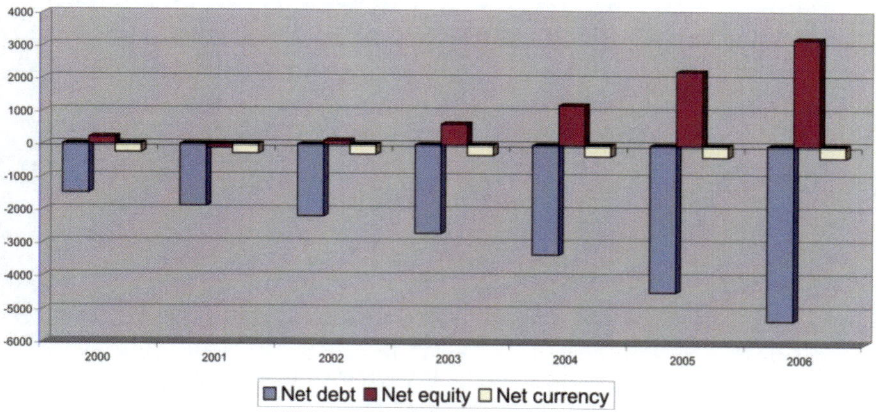

Chart 2. Rising market value of US FDI/ Equity invesment abroad has offset much of the increase in US external debt (data BEA, $ billion)

The improvement in the US net equity position largely reflects capital gains on existing US equity investment, not large (net) US purchase of foreign equities.[2] Since the end of 2000:

Foreign equity markets generally outperformed the US equity market in local currency terms.

The dollar's slide against European currencies and the Canadian dollar has substantially increased dollar value of existing investment in Europe and Canada.

Indeed, the capital gains on US equity investment abroad since 2002 have been large enough to entirely offset the increase in debt associated with the current account deficit, so the US net international investment position hasn't deteriorated.

The income balance – the gap between the interest and dividends that the US pays to the rest of the world and the interest and dividends that the US receives from the rest of the world — also has not deteriorated as rapidly as many had feared. The revised data from Bureau of Economic Analysis (BEA) indicates that the US actually received more interest and dividend income from the rest of the world than it paid out in 2006 (Chart 3).

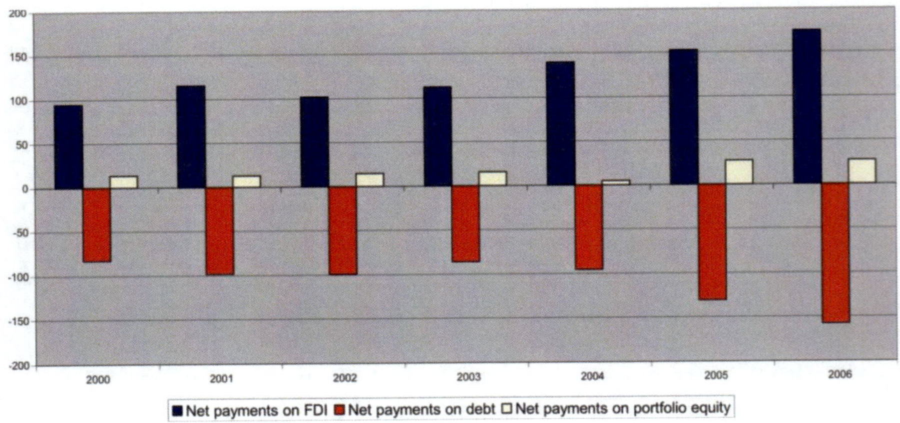

Chart 3. The US income balance: $ billion, BEA data.

Here too the overall balance can be disaggregated into the interest payments on debt and the dividends payments on equity. As one would expect, payments on US external debt have increased substantially. Interest payments on US external debt likely totaled $430b in 2006, up from a low of $170b in 2003 and $250b in 2000 (Chart 4).[3] This trend continued in the first quarter of 2007: the q1 data suggests the 2007 US interest bill will be substantially higher than $500b. However, interest income on US lending abroad – which seems to be primarily short-term –also has increased. Right now, the implied interest rate on US lending is close to 6%, while the implied interest rate on US borrowing is close to 4.5% (Chart 5). In my judgment, this large gap is unlikely to persist. As the average interest rate on the United States (large) stock of external debt rises, the US income balance should begin to deteriorate.

The US income balance has also been helped by a large ongoing gap between the reported dividend income of US direct investment abroad and foreign direct investment in the US, a gap that stems more from low reported returns on foreign direct investment in the US than high reported returns on US direct investment abroad (Chart 6).

The ability of the United States to run large deficits without much deterioration in its net international investment position or a significant deterioration in its income deficit reflects the willingness of the United States' external creditors to add to their holdings of US debt when — at least in retrospect – they would have received far larger financial returns had they invested in foreign equities. Foreigners would have fared better if they had forced the US to sell its existing external assets rather just buying US debt.

THE ROLE OF FOREIGN CENTRAL BANKS

No one doubts that foreign central banks – including the People's Bank of China – have been very large buyers of US debt securities. The BEA data show that official purchases of US assets rose from under $100b a year in 2000 and 2001 to nearly $400b in 2004. Official inflows then fell to $275b in 2005 – a year when rising US short-term rates and the Homeland Investment

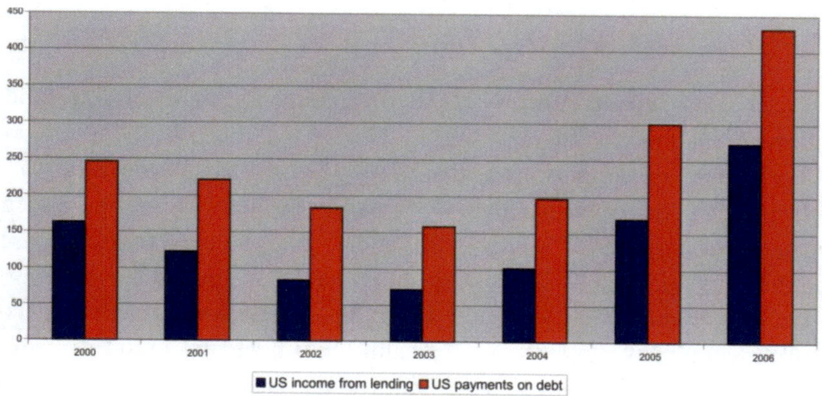

Chart 4. Interest payments and receipts: $ billion, BEA data.

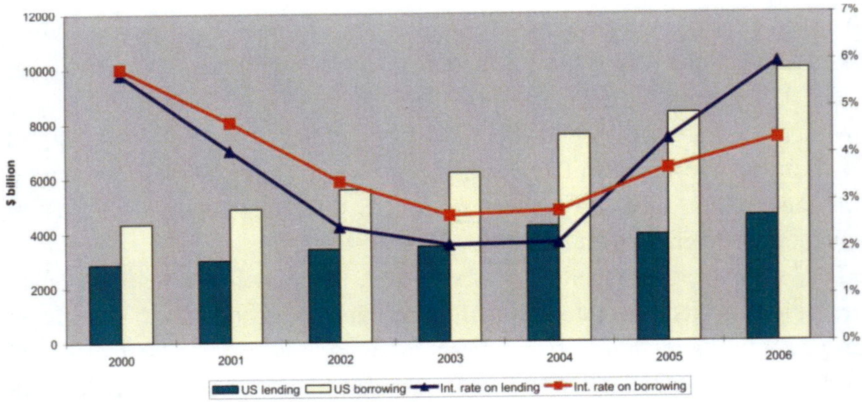

Chart 5. Interest rate differentials matter ...

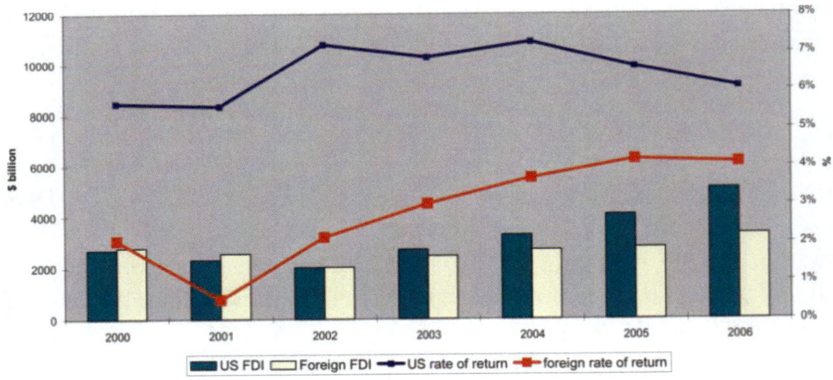

Chart 6. Stock/ Returns on FDI.

Act helped support the dollar – before rising to $440b in 2006 and an annualized $600b in the first quarter of 2006.

Large as these inflows are – the $440b in central bank purchases of US assets in 2006 far exceeded the $155b in marketable Treasuries issued to finance the US fiscal deficit in 2006, and the large cumulative increase in central bank holdings of Treasuries since 2000 has limited the increase in marketable treasuries held privately (Chart 7) – the BEA data likely understate the role central banks and sovereign wealth funds have played in financing the US external deficit. The BEA data do not capture the dollars that central banks have on deposit in banks outside the US. Those dollars are then lent out, and indirectly help to increase private demand for dollar-denominated debt, including US dollar denominated debt.[4] Most importantly, recent BEA data do not capture large central bank purchases of US assets made through private custodians in London and other financial centers. The BEA's data is revised annually to reflect the information provided by United States Treasury's annual survey of foreign portfolio investment in the US, which tends to do a better, though still imperfect, [5]job of capturing the ultimate ownership of US debt securities. However, the most recent data points tend to substantially understate central bank purchases of US assets.

A number of technical difficulties complicate efforts to determine the exact impact of central bank demand for US debt on US yields. Custodial bias makes real-time estimates of the size of official inflows hard. The shift in central bank demand from Treasuries to Agencies after 2005 further complicates analysis. But many studies find a substantial impact – 100 to 150bp at the peak of central bank demand for US assets in 2004 (Warnock and Warnock, 2005, Moec and Frey, 2005). When the analysis of the recently revised data – which shows far higher central bank purchases in 2006 than the BEA had previously indicated – is completed, I would expect to find that central banks exerted a similar impact in 2006.

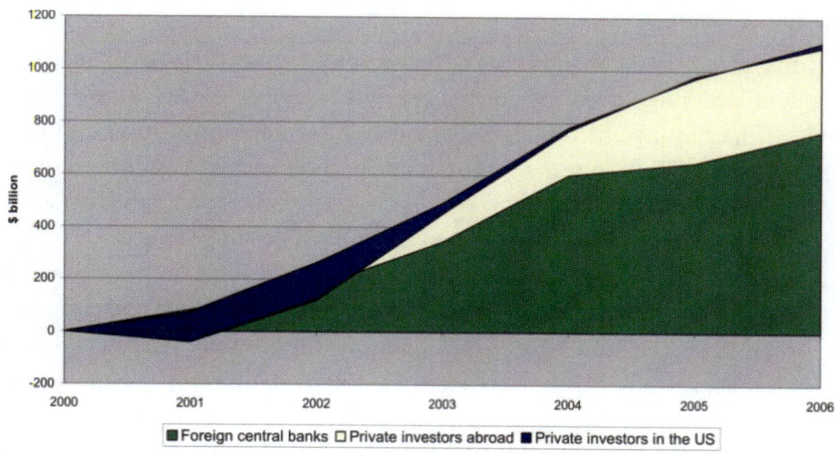

Chart 7. Cumulative increase in the stock of marketable Treasuries not held by the Fed since 2000 (Flow of funds data, this data has not been revised to reflect the latest survey, so it overstates private holdings abroad and understates central bank holdings)

Central bank demand for US debt, generally speaking, has allowed the US to finance a larger deficit at lower cost than otherwise would have been the case. Assessing the longterm impact of these policies on the overall US economy is difficult, since strong demand for debt securities and low interest rates help some sectors even as other sectors are hurt by other countries efforts to keep their currencies under-valued.

Central bank demand for US debt has helped lower the interest burden of the US government. It has encouraged heavy household borrowing, both to support consumption growth in excess of income growth and – between 2003 and 2006 — a surge in residential investment. More recently, low interest rates have supported strong demand for corporate debt, whether from firms looking to buy back their equity (and thus push up their stock price) or private equity firms, which borrow heavily to buy the listed stock of publicly traded companies.[6] Conversely, those sectors of the US economy that compete with imports, particularly imports from emerging economies, and that export goods and services have been hurt by the policies that gave rise to these large official inflows.

In aggregate, I believe the negative long-term impacts of the policies that have given rise to large official inflows to the US outweigh the positive. While many in the US clearly have gained from low interest rates, it is hard to argue that the US has been borrowing from abroad to invest in ways that will generate the future export revenue needed to repay the United States' growing external debt. Suburban housing is not an obvious source of export revenue – and firms that borrow to buy back their equity rather than to finance new investment are not obviously increasing the United States' future export capacity either. Many abroad have also gained from their government's efforts to prop up the dollar – not the least China's export sector. But these policies will also generate losers, notably taxpayers in emerging economies who will at some point incur large losses on their government's dollar holdings.

Nonetheless, it is important to recognize that central banks have generally acted to stabilize rather than to destabilize the foreign exchange and bond markets. Since early 2004, the IMF's data on central bank reserves indicate that central banks effectively have bought dollars – and dollar-denominated bonds – when private market participants have been unwilling to do so, helping to stabilize US and global financial markets. As a result, a fall off in (net) private demand for US assets has not let to a large drop in overall foreign demand for US assets, allowing the US to finance its large deficit at a relatively low costs. Volatility in private demand for US assets has translated into volatility in central bank dollar reserve growth, not volatility in financial markets or in aggregate financial flows to the US.

This has been particularly apparent over the last three quarters. As the US economy slowed and growth abroad picked-up, net private capital inflows to the US fell. US demand for foreign assets rose, and demand for US assets from private investors abroad fell. The BEA's data, for example, show for q1 that central banks provided about $150b in direct financing to the US in the first quarter – a net inflow equal to about 75% of the US current account deficit.

The $150b in official inflows in q1 is if anything an under-estimation of likely central bank financing of the US in the first quarter. The high-frequency data released by the US (The monthly Treasury International capital data and the quarterly BEA balance of payments data) tend to overstate private purchases and understate official purchases. Lower frequency data – notably the United States annual survey of foreign portfolio investment – tends to do a better job of picking-up central bank purchases of US assets.

The last survey – which covered the period between June 2005 and June 2006 – showed $345 in official purchases of long-term US debt, $125b more than in the unrevised data. The last survey, for example, revised the United States estimate of Chinese purchases of US debt up by $90b. (See Chart 8; Chinese holdings of US Treasuries jump every June, when the survey data is released). There is no reason to think that this pattern will change.[7]

I consequently prefer high-frequency estimates of the increase in central bank dollar holdings that are derived from reported increase in foreign central bank reserves, along with an estimate of the share of those reserves that are held in dollars. This methodology has its limits. It will, for example, over-estimate central bank purchases of dollars if central banks are reducing the dollar's share of their reserves. Nonetheless, this methodology accurately predicted the large upward revisions in central bank holdings in the last survey (see Charts 9 and 10).

With total global reserve growth topping $250b in q1, this methodology implies that central bank demand for dollar assets now tops $200b a quarter. Preliminary data for q2 suggests global reserve growth will top $300b by a substantial margin, which implies a truly extraordinary $250b in central bank demand for dollar assets in q2. The very strong recent growth in the New York Fed's custodial holdings – which have been running at an annualized pace of close to $500b this year – provide strong indirect evidence of a strong rise in US dependence on inflows from foreign central banks (Chart 11).

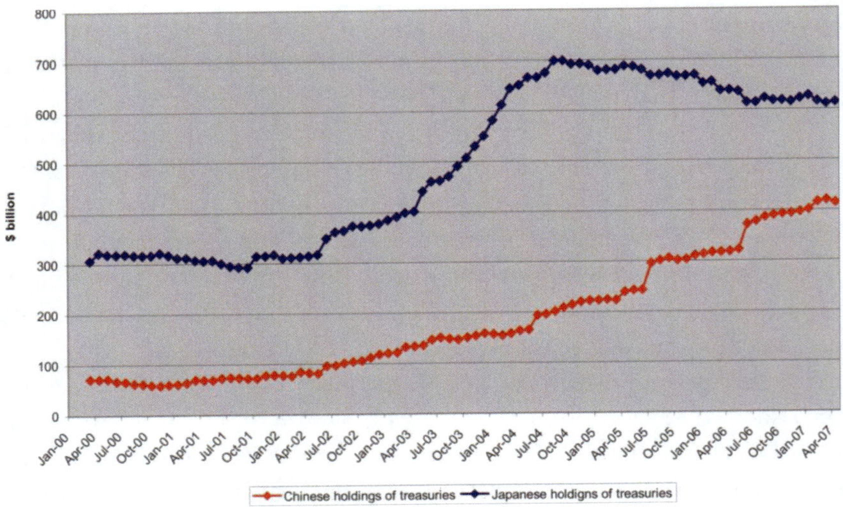

Chart 8. Chinese and Japanese holdings of Treasuries

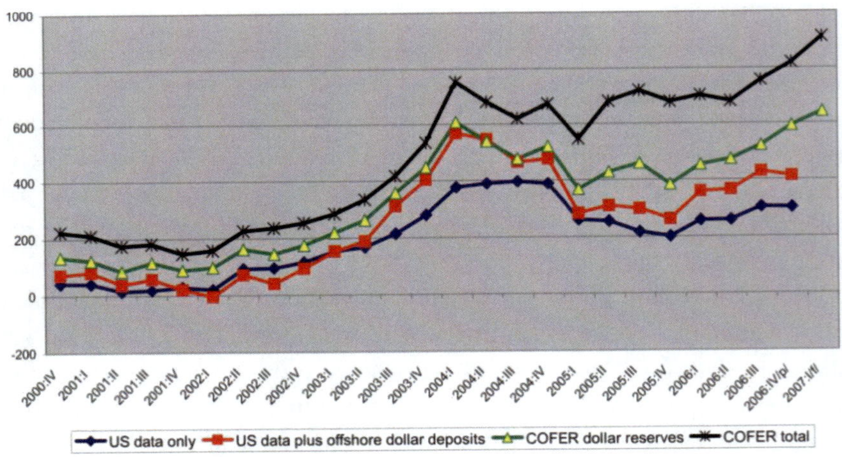

Chart 9. Prior to the latest revisions, measured offiical inflows are lower than estimates derived from the IMF (COFER) data Rolling 4 quarter sums, $ billion

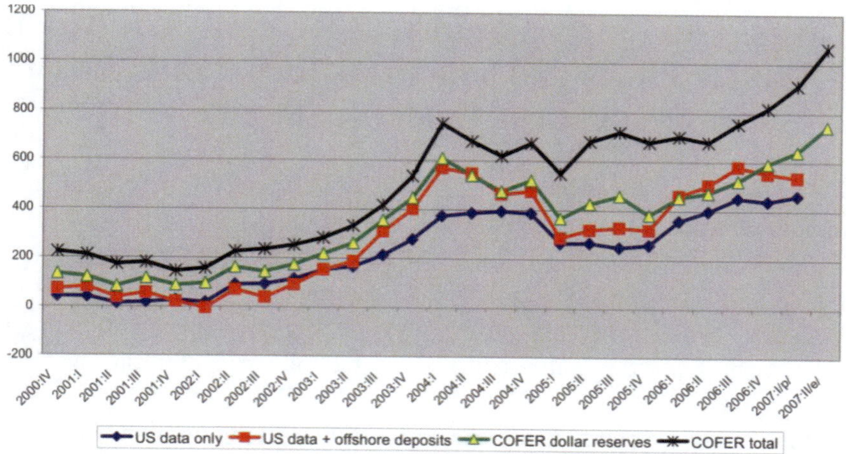

Chart 10. After the latest data revisions, recored inflows now match estimates derived from the IMF (COFER) data, $ billion, rolling four quarter sums

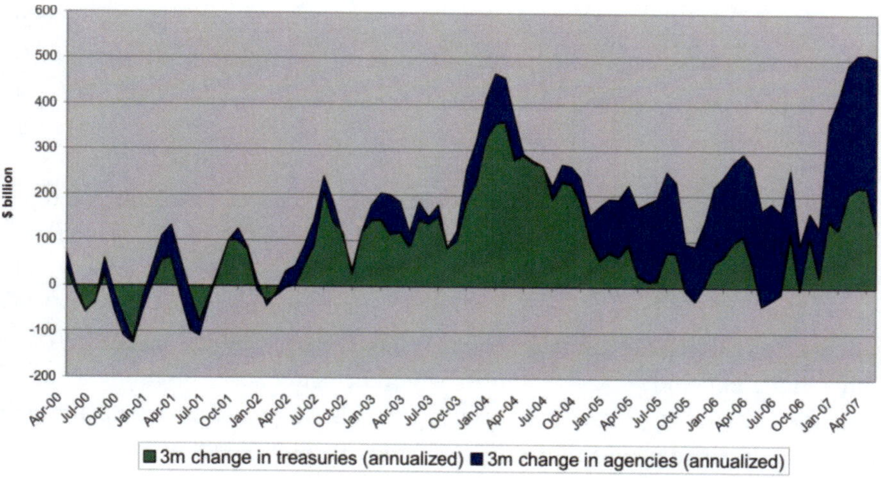

Chart 11. Record growth in foreign central banks custodial accounts at the New York Fed Rolling 3m sums, annualized

RISKS: TOO LITTLE OFFICIAL FINANCING, TOO MUCH OFFICIAL FINANCING AND MORE DEMANDING TERMS FROM THE OFFICIAL SECTOR

Ongoing US dependence on central bank demand for US assets carries with it three risks:

Central banks stop adding to the dollar holdings.

Central banks resist all market pressure for adjustment, allowing the underlying disequilibrium – and total foreign claims on the US, to build.

Foreign governments change the terms of their financing of the US.

Professor Rogoff, a fellow member of this panel, has argued that the large credit line extended by emerging economy central banks to the US constitutes a kind of reverse foreign aid. Both relatively poor emerging economies and wealthy oil exporting economies that are intervening heavily to keep their exchange rates from appreciating are effectively "over-paying" for US dollar-denominated assets. Should they stop intervening, their exchange rates will rise – reducing the value of their existing dollar holdings in local currency terms.

The resulting losses potentially are quite significant. Chinese intervention in the foreign exchange market is currently close to 15% of its GDP. If the RMB is undervalued by 33% against a basket of euros and dollars that corresponds with China's foreign currency reserves, the annual cost of this policy is roughly 5% of China's GDP.[8] It is possible – though unlikely -- that China might conclude that its interests would be better served running a 5% of GDP fiscal deficit to finance a social security system and better health care rather than incurring an expected loss of 5% of its GDP lending to the US and Europe. Of course, the effective subsidy that China extends to American borrowers also benefits China's export sector – there are strong interests inside China that seek to maintain the current policy. However, those who depend on the kindness of strangers shouldn't take their continued kindness for granted.

Emerging economies do not need to sell their existing reserves to shake the system –all they need to do is stop adding to their dollar reserves/ dollar assets of their investment funds. Indeed, if emerging markets just held their purchases of US assets constant at a time when private demand for US assets fell, they could have a substantial impact on US financial markets. The markets now expect that emerging economy central banks will be the dollar's buyer of last resort.

China is the largest single source of financing for the US external deficit. China probably accounted for about 1/3 of all long-term debt purchased by foreigners in 2006, and more like ½ of all foreign purchases of Treasuries and Agencies. The strong increase in the pace of Chinese reserve growth implies that China will likely account for a higher share of total purchases in 2007. Changes in how China allocates its immense and rapidly growing portfolio consequently could have a large impact on US markets. A reduction in Chinese purchases of all US debt would have the largest impact, but even shifts in the kinds of assets that China buys now could have a substantial impact. For all the attention that China's $3b investment in Blackstone generated, it likely represents less than one week's worth of Chinese purchases of debt.

China is not the only actor with the potential to shock the US financial system. The Institute for International Finance recently reported that the oil-exporting economies of the Gulf have more accumulated foreign assets than China. They also hold nearly as large a share of their assets in dollars, even though only 10% of their imports come from the US. Should the Gulf states change the dollar's share of their portfolio suddenly, they too could potentially put substantial pressure on the dollar.

This risk isn't new. Back in 2003, Former Treasury Secretary Lawrence Summers warned that the United States dependence on credit from countries selling goods to the US was generating "a balance of financial terror": the US was dependent on China for large-scale financing, while China depended on the US to provide sufficient demand for its products. More recently, Summers noted that one lesson of the cold war is that a system based on a balance of terror can be stable for quite some time.

However, the system's current apparent stability is in some ways deceiving, as the costs emerging economies are being asked to bear to sustain the United States existing current account deficit are rising. Emerging market reserve growth has doubled since early 2006, rising from around $600b to around $1.2 trillion, as private investors shifted funds from the US to the emerging world. To be sure, large scale reserve growth generates benefits for exporters in emerging economies. But rapid reserve growth also limits the domestic monetary policy autonomy of many emerging economies, as well as generating financial losses – now generally hidden – that taxpayers in emerging economies will eventually have to absorb. The constellation of interests that supports the status quo may not last forever. At some point, the perceived costs of buying dollars when the dollar is under pressure may exceed the perceived benefits that emerging market economies gain from resisting market pressures for appreciation.

One risk is that emerging economies suddenly stop adding to their dollar holdings, forcing the US to adjust to fall off in foreign financing too rapidly. Another risk, ironically, is that emerging economies will continue to add to their reserves at a pace that allows the US to continue to defer a necessary adjustment.

Substantial swings in the private sector's willingness to finance US external deficits – and a large gap between the size of the US deficit and net private inflows in 2003, 2004, 2006 and so far in 2007 — have not translated into large swings in the US external accounts or sharp swings in US economic activity. However, strong central bank demand for US debt – a byproduct of their decision to resist market pressure for their currencies to appreciate – risks thwarting all adjustment, not just thwarting disruptive adjustment.

If the US trade deficit remains constant as a share of GDP, the deterioration in the US income balance associated with a rising stock of external claims on the US implies a growing current account deficit over time. The Congressional Budget Office's recent analysis of the US external deficit accurately noted that a sharp adjustment process would bring the US deficit down quickly, limiting the overall increase in US net external indebtedness. By contrast, a period without any adjustment – or a further rise in the US external deficit – that is followed by a period of gradual adjustment implies that the overall US external debt stock would rise even further than would be the case if the US deficit started to fall now.

This risk is not entirely theoretical. The recent slowdown in US growth – combined with an acceleration in global growth – created close to ideal conditions for the US external deficit to fall. Strong global growth supported US exports. The slowdown in US growth slowed the increase in US imports. Indeed, the US deficit with those regions of the world – Europe and North America – that have allowed their currencies to appreciate has fallen substantially. However, the US deficit with East Asia continues to rise (Chart 12). At a result, the fall in the United States overall deficit has been modest. Most of the improvement in the current account deficit from its recent peak in the third quarter of 2006 stems from lower oil prices.

A final risk that is worth noting: the rest of the world may change the terms associated with its financing.

Countries like China have resisted taking policy steps – like faster RMB appreciation or a major initiative to stimulate domestic consumption – that would lower their current account surplus and reduce the scale of their purchase of US assets. However, such countries are clearly seeking to invest in US assets that offer the prospect for greater returns than US Treasuries.

Such an evolution is natural. China holds far more liquid Treasury and Agency securities than it needs to address even a most draconian shock. Moreover, China's heavy concentration in US fixed income securities (Chart 13)[9] is itself a risk. A rise in Chinese holdings of US equities is a natural by-product of China's large surplus, the United States large deficit and a balanced Chinese portfolio of US assets. China's willingness to hold such a high share of its national wealth in low-yielding debt is far more unusual than its interest in exploring alternatives that offer higher potential returns.

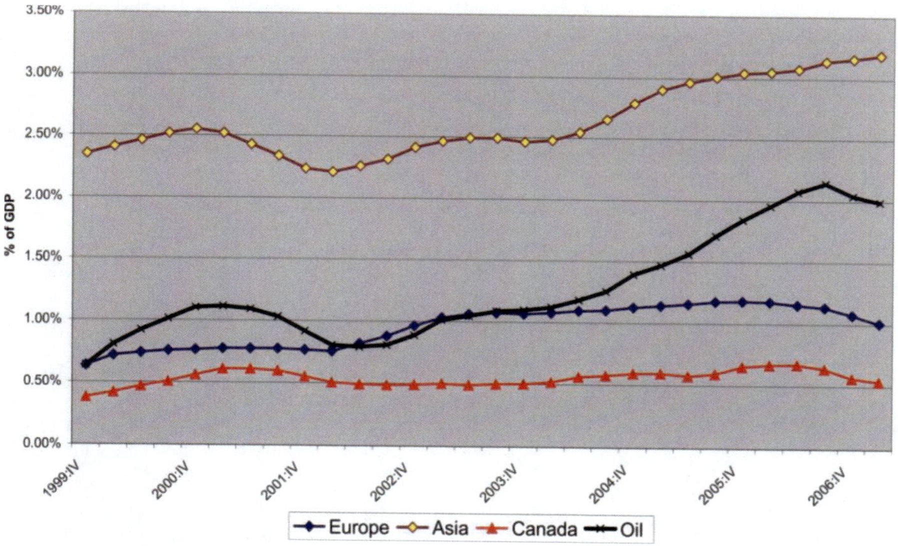

Chart 12. US goods trade balance with key regions of the world (rolling four quarter total, as a % of US GDP)

The current pace of accumulation of Chinese foreign assets suggests that China's total foreign assets will rise from about $1.5 trillion at the end of 2006 (with about 1.2 trillion of that reserves and reserves-like assets) to more than $3 trillion by 2010. A world where China creates a $1.5 trillion dollar investment fund, rather than adds $1.5 trillion to its reserves, over the next few years isn't impossible to envision. Even if China adds roughly equal sums to its reserves and investment fund over the next few years (Chart 14), its investment fund could reach be the largest in the world by 2010. Creating an investment fund won't eliminate the constraints on China's overall portfolio that stem from China's continued adherence to its dollar peg. However, shifts in the kind of assets that China is purchasing could still influence US markets. A Chinese move away from long-term fixed-income debt could increase US interest rates by as much as 50 basis points.

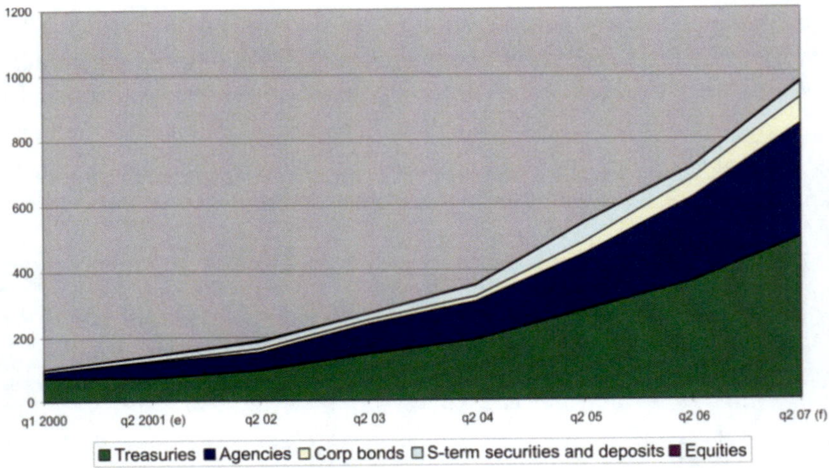

Chart 13. Reported Chinese holdings of US assets: US suvery data; 2007 = estimate

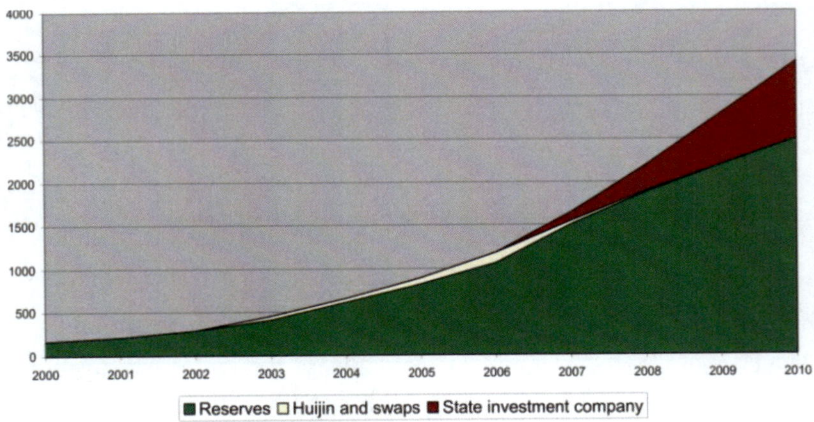

Chart 14. Distribution of Chinese foreign assets over time? 2007-2010 assumes stable $500b increase in foreign assets

Other central banks now adding to the reserves rapidly (Russia) and other central banks with large existing stocks of reserves (Korea and Japan) have either announced that they are creating a new investment fund (Russia, Korea)

or are rumored to be considering an investment fund (Japan). All seem to be struck by the high returns Singapore has obtained from its investment funds. So long as oil prices remain high, the assets of existing investment funds in Norway will continue to grow as well. All these funds already hold substantial quantities of US equities, both directly and through their investment in private equity and hedge funds.

Trying to shut the investment funds of foreign governments out of US markets is neither feasible nor desirable. So long as the United States is running large external deficits, US government is unlikely to be in a position where it will be able to dictate what kind of U.S. assets its creditors are allowed to buy. Moreover, any move to shut government investment funds out of the US market would invite foreign governments to try to limit US investment in their markets.

Nonetheless, the growing presence of government investment funds in US equity markets raises a host of questions – questions about US capital market regulation as well as questions about the transparency of large investment funds. Edwin Truman of the Peterson Institute has argued that the increased role of central banks and sovereign wealth funds in global capital markets implies that both should adhere to a higher level of transparency. He specifically has called for more disclosure of their investment strategies as well as the currency composition of their portfolios. I second Dr. Truman's suggestion, along with a recent suggestion from the Treasury's Acting Under Secretary, Clay Lowery, that the IMF encourage investment funds to develop a code of best practices.

CONCLUSION

So long as the US is running a large external deficit, foreign holdings of US assets will need to rise faster than US holdings of foreign assets. In many ways, the past few years have been atypical. The United States' external deficit has been financed entirely by the net sale of debt securities rather than by the net sale of equities, in no small part because of unprecedented growth in central bank reserve assets. The low interest rate on US external debt – relative to both the returns the US has achieved on its equity investment and the interest rate on US external lending – has allowed the US to continue to earn more on its foreign investment than it pays on its foreign debts.

These patterns are unlikely to persist. So long as emerging economies are unwilling to allow their currencies to appreciate and run large current account surpluses – especially with private capital flowing in net into emerging economies – many governments around the world will be accumulating external asset rapidly. Over time, though, more of those assets will be handed over investment funds and fewer will be held as central bank reserves. The US will likely both have to sell more equity to the rest of the world and pay a somewhat higher interest rate on its external debt than it has recently.

Foreign investors – and right now that means foreign governments – now finance, directly and indirectly, a larger share of domestic US investment than makes sense over time. While rapid central bank reserve growth and large official financing of the US deficit can help the US postpone the necessary adjustment, the longer the adjustment is deferred, the greater the long-term risks.

The process of adjustment is more likely to be smooth if it is supported both by policy changes here in the US and abroad. The US government should adopt policies that would allow the US to finance more investment out of domestic US savings, just as many emerging economies should put more of their savings to work at home. Further reduction in the fiscal deficit and a new push to reduce our energy import bill – the United States "petroleum" deficit is now close to $300b – are the most obvious policies for the United States. Governments in emerging markets need to do more than complain about US profligacy, particularly when their purchases of US debt have masked the consequences of the United States' low level of savings and large resulting external deficit. East Asian economies with high savings rates – notably China – have substantial scope to take policy steps to support domestic consumption. Most governments that now manage their exchange rate against the dollar – whether in the Gulf, Latin America or East Asia — would benefit from additional exchange rate flexibility.

Both the United States large deficit and equally large surpluses in many emerging economies built up gradually over time. Bringing the US deficit and emerging economy surpluses down without tremendous costs will also take time. If the US and the world are to adjust gradually, they need to get started.

ENDNOTES

[1] The US has not formally released data on the total stock of foreign claims on the US for the end of 2006. I have drawn on the data from the 2005 net international investment position, the

2006 capital account data from the Bureau of Economic Analysis, the 2006 Treasury survey of foreign portfolio investment in the US and China's reserves data to compile these estimates. The actual data should be released at the end of June.

[2] Since the end of 2000, cumulative US direct investment abroad has exceeded foreign direct investment in the US by about $200b. Portfolio equity inflows and outflows are roughly equal.

[3] These estimates are derived from the balance of payments data released by the Bureau of Economic Analysis. The exact number for 2006 though depends on dividend payments on foreign portfolio investment in the US – a data point that the BEA has yet to release. I assumed that 2006 dividend payments matched 2005 dividend payments. Since these payments are small, this is not a large source of error.

[4] Foreign central banks purchases of euro and pound denominated securities also help to generate indirect demand for US debt, as such purchases push down European yields and make US assets relatively more attractive to private investors in the US and Europe.

[5] The survey data seems to understate the Middle East's likely holdings of US assets, perhaps because neither the high-frequency data BEA data (which is derived from the Treasury's TIC data) nor the annual survey picks up foreign central bank funds – and sovereign wealth funds – that are managed by private portfolio managers.

[6] Central banks are not large direct participants in this market but by lowering yields in Treasury and Agency bonds (and buying these bonds from pension funds and other investors) they encouraged other investors to reach for yield. Significant central bank deposits in the international banking system have also supported the leveraged loan market.

[7] In the first quarter of 2007, the increase in the New York Federal Reserve Bank's custodial holdings of US treasury and US Agency bonds exceeded the estimated increase in central bank holdings of US treasury and US Agency bonds in the BEA's balance of payments data by about $20b. Central banks who buy US securities in London sometimes hand those securities over to the New York fed; the transfer of custodianship though is not considered a sale.

[8] This calculation ignores the "carry" the Chinese government gets from borrowing at low interest rates in China to buy US dollar debt. It is clear, though, that these interest gains – which themselves stem from China's artificially low interest rates – are not large enough to offset the capital losses from a substantial RMB appreciation. China's reserves are now roughly 45% of its GDP. China's central bank will eventually face a loss equal to 15% of China's GDP.

[9] The best data on China's holdings of US assets comes from the annual US survey of foreign portfolio investment. As of June, 2006, China held slightly a bit under $700b in US debt: $375b of US Treasury bills and notes, $260b of "agency" bonds, and $60b of corporate debt. In addition, China held slightly over $20b of US equities – and a bit over $15b in plain old bank deposits. . Treasuries and Agencies accounted for 90% of all Chinese holdings of US securities, debt securities accounted for 99.5% of China's US portfolio (Chart 5) and US securities accounted for around 70% of China's total reserves (included reserves shifted to the state banks. The US data does not distinguish between US assets held by China's private sector (including its state commercial banks) and US assets held by China's State Administration of Foreign Exchange. However, given the size of China's reserves, it is reasonably to assume that the State Administration of Foreign Exchange accounts for most of China's recorded holdings of US securities.

In: Foreign Investment In U.S. Securities
Editors: Declan J. Byrne
ISBN: 978-1-60876-084-8

Chapter 3

FOREIGN INVESTMENTS IN U.S. SECURITIES

James K. Jackson

SUMMARY

Foreign capital inflows are playing an important role in the U.S. economy by bridging the gap between domestic supplies of and demand for capital. In 2008, as the financial crisis and global economic downturn unfolded, foreign investors looked to U.S. Treasury securities as a "safe haven" investment, while they sharply reduced their net purchases of corporate stocks and bonds. Foreign investors now hold more than 50% of the publicly held and traded U.S. Treasury securities. The large foreign accumulation of U.S. securities has spurred some observers to arguethat this large foreign presence in U.S. financial markets increases the risk of a financial crisis, whether as a result of the uncoordinated actions of market participants or by a coordinated withdrawal from U.S. financial markets by foreign investors for economic or political reasons.

Congress likely would find itself embroiled in any such financial crisis through its direct role in conducting fiscal policy and in its indirect role in the conduct of monetary policy through its supervisory responsibility over the Federal Reserve. Such a coordinated withdrawal seems highly unlikely, particularly since the vast majority of the investors are private entities that presumably would find it difficult to coordinate a withdrawal. The financial crisis and economic downturn, however, have sharply reduced the value of the assets foreign investors acquired, which may make them more hesitant in the future to invest in certain types of securities. As a result of the financial crisis of 2008, foreign investors curtailed their purchases of corporate securities, a phenomenon that was not unique to the United States. In a sense, the slowdown in the U.S. economy and rise in personal savings have eased somewhat the need for foreign investment. The importance of capital inflows may well change as the federal government's budget deficits rise over the course of the economic downturn.. This report analyzes the extent of foreign portfolio investment in the U.S. economy and assesses the economic conditions that are attracting such investment and the impact such investments are having on the economy.

Economists generally attribute this rise in foreign investment to a number of factors, including: "safe haven" investment during times of uncertainty; comparatively favorable returns on investments, a surplus of saving in other areas of the world, the well-developed U.S. financial system, and the overall stability and rate of growth of the U.S. economy. Capital inflows also allow the United States to finance its trade deficit because foreigners are willing to lend to the United States in the form of exchanging the sale of goods, represented by U.S. imports, for such U.S. assets as U.S. businesses and real estate, stocks, bonds, and U.S. Treasury securities. Despite improvements in capital mobility, foreign capital inflows do not fully replace or compensate for a lack of domestic sources of capital. Economic analysis shows that a nation's rate of capital formation, or domestic investment, seems to have been linked primarily to its domestic rate of saving.

This report relies on a comprehensive set of data on capital flows, represented by purchases and sales of U.S. government securities and U.S. and foreign corporate stocks, bonds, into and out of the United States, that is reported by the Treasury Department on a monthly basis. This report will updated as events warrant.

Foreign capital inflows play an important role in the U.S. economy by bridging the gap between domestic supplies of and demand for capital. The importance of these flows has been underscored by the financial crisis in 2008, when international capital markets essentially shut down for a period of time. International capital flows and international capital markets also generally give the owners of capital the ability to reduce their risk by diversifying their investments. Oversight of these markets likely will change as a result of the financial crisis. Foreign investors currently own more than 50% of the publicly held and traded U.S. Treasury securities and hold large amounts of U.S. corporate stocks and bonds, although the value of these assets has dropped markedly. Capital inflows help keep U.S. interest rates below the level they would reach without them and have allowed the nation to spend beyond its current output, including financing its trade deficit. Some observers have expressed concerns about the extent of these foreign holdings, because they argue that this exposure increases the overall risks to the economy should foreign investors decide to withdraw from the U.S. financial markets for political or economic reasons. At the same time, the funding requirements of the U.S. economy may temper the criticism of some foreign investors, especially if capital flows should shrink and U.S. funding requirements increase.

Inflows of capital into the U.S. economy are not new, although they grew sporadically over the last decade, as indicated in **Table 1**. In 1996, total foreign capital inflows to the United States reached over $551 billion. As **Figure 1** shows, these capital inflows are comprised of official inflows, primarily foreign governments' purchases of U.S. Treasury securities, and private inflows comprised of portfolio investment, which includes foreigners' purchases of U.S. Treasury and corporate securities, and financial liabilities, and direct investment in U.S. businesses and real estate. By 2000, total foreign capital inflows totaled more than $1 trillion. Such inflows were reduced in 2001 and 2002 as the growth rate of the U.S. economy slowed, but grew to over $2.0 trillion in 2007 as the rate of economic growth improved. Private capital inflows comprise more than three-fourths of the total capital inflows, with foreign purchases of corporate securities, stocks and bonds being the main components of these inflows. In 2007, official inflows are estimated to account for 17% of total foreign capital inflows, down from 23.7% in 2006.

Capital flows are highly liquid, can respond abruptly to changes in economic and financial conditions, and exercise a primary influence on exchange rates and through those on global flows of goods and services. Economists generally attribute this rise in foreign investment to a number of factors, including a "safe haven" effect during times of uncertainty; comparatively favorable returns on investments relative to risk, a surplus of saving in other areas of the world, the welldeveloped U.S. financial system, and the overall stability of the U.S. economy. These net capital inflows (inflows net of outflows) bridge the gap in the United States between the amount of credit demanded and the domestic supply of funds, likely keeping U.S. interest rates below the level they would have reached without the foreign capital. These capital inflows also allow the United States to spend beyond its means, including financing its trade deficit, because foreigners are willing to lend to the United States in the form of exchanging goods, represented by U.S. imports, for such U.S. assets as stocks, bonds, and U.S. Treasury securities.

Table 1. Capital Inflows to the United States, 1996-2007 (in billions of dollars)

	Total	Official assets	Private assets					
			Total	Direct investment	Treasury securities	Corporate securities	U.S. currency	Other
1996	($)551.1	($)126.7	($)424.4	($)86.5	($)147.0	($)103.3	($)17.4	($)70.2
1997	706.8	19.0	687.8	105.6	130.4	161.4	24.8	265.5
1998	423.6	-19.9	443.5	179.0	28.6	156.3	16.6	62.9
1999	740.2	43.5	696.7	289.4	-44.5	298.8	22.4	130.5
2000	1,046.9	42.8	1,004.1	321.3	-70.0	459.9	5.3	287.6
2001	782.9	28.1	754.8	167.0	-14.4	393.9	23.8	184.5
2002	768.2	114.0	654.3	72.4	100.4	285.5	21.5	174.4
2003	829.2	248.6	580.6	39.9	113.4	251.0	16.6	159.7
2004	1,440.1	394.7	1,045.4	106.8	107.0	369.8	14.8	477.0
2005	1,204.2	259.3	995.0	109.0	132.3	450.4	19.0	234.3
2006	1,859.6	440.3	1,419.3	180.6	-35.9	592.0	12.6	670.2
2007	2,057.7	411.1	1,646.6	237.5	156.8	573.9	10.7	689.1

Source: Weinberg, Douglas, and Renee M. Sauers, U.S. International Transactions, Third Quarter of 2008, *Survey of Current Business*, January, 2009. p.36.

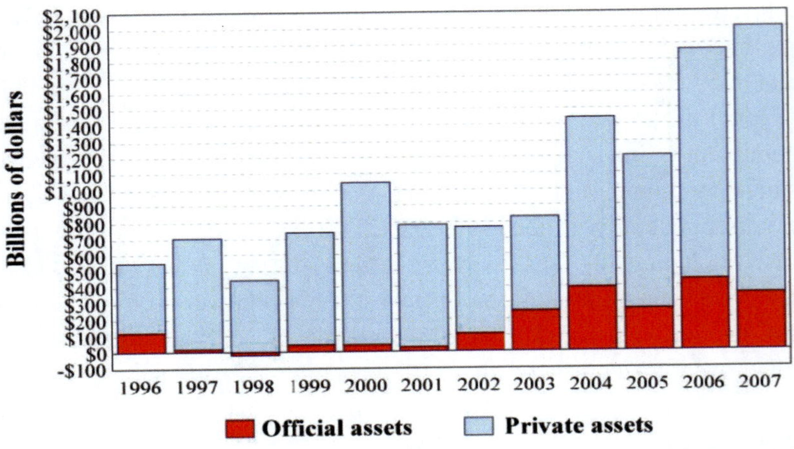

Figure 1. Foreign Official and Private Capital Inflows to the United States, 1996-2007
Source: Department of Commerce

CAPITAL FLOWS IN THE ECONOMY

Table 2 shows the net flow of funds in the U.S. economy. The flow of funds accounts measure financial flows across sectors of the economy, tracking funds as they move from those sectors that supply the sources of capital through intermediaries to sectors that use the capital to acquire physical and financial assets.[1] The net flows show the overall financial position by sector, whether that sector is a net supplier or a net user of financial capital in the economy. Since the demand for funds in the economy as a whole must equal the supply of funds, a deficit in one sector must be offset by a surplus in another sector. Generally, the household sector, or individuals, provides funds to the economy, because individuals save part of their income, while the business sector uses those funds to invest in plant and equipment that, in turn, serve as the building blocks for the production of additional goods and services. The Government sector (the combination of federal, state, and local governments) can be either a net supplier of funds or a net user depending on whether the sector is running a surplus or a deficit, respectively. The interplay within the economy between saving and investment, or the supply and uses of funds, tends to affect domestic interest rates, which move to equate the demand and supply of funds. Shifts in the interest rate also tend to attract capital from abroad, denoted by the rest of the world (ROW) in **Table 2**.

As **Table 2** indicates, from 1996 through 1998, the household sector ran a net surplus, or provided net savings to the economy. The business sector also provided net surplus funds in 1996, or businesses earned more in profits than they invested. The government sector, primarily the federal government, experienced net deficits, which decreased until 1998, when the federal government and state and local governments experienced financial surpluses. Capital inflows from the rest of the world rose and fell during this period, depending on the combination of household saving, business sector saving and investment, and the extent of the deficit or surplus in the government sector.

Starting in 1999, the household sector began dissaving, as individuals spent more than they earned. Part of this dissaving was offset by the government sector, which experienced a surplus from 1998 to 2001. As a result of the large household dissaving, however, the economy as a whole experienced a gap between domestic saving and investment that was filled with large capital inflows. Those inflows were particularly large in nominal terms from 2000 to 2006 as household dissaving continued and government sector surpluses turned to historically large deficits in nominal terms.

Capital inflows in 2008 were $611 billion, about $160 billion less than that recorded in 2007. This drop in capital inflows reflected a sharp reversal in the behavior of households from dissaving to saving, an increase in business sector dissaving, and an increase in the deficits experienced by state and local governments as the effects of the slowdown in the economy became more pronounced. Households turned from a dissaving of $100 billion in 2007 to a net saving of $520 billion in 2008, reflecting the growing concern among households over the state of the economy. The Federal Reserve reported that in 2008, households experienced a drop in their net worth of more than $11 trillion, or about 20%.[2]

Table 2. Flow of Funds of the U.S. Economy, 1996-2008 (in billions of dollars)

Year	Households	Businesses	Government			ROW
			Total	State and Local	Federal	
1996	175.2	19.8	-196.8	-1.2	-195.6	137.9
1997	47.4	-18.3	-116.6	-47.5	-69.1	219.6
1998	128.0	-45.7	64.8	48.8	16.0	75.0
1999	-132.7	-62.6	115.3	9.9	105.4	231.7
2000	-371.0	-82.9	252.5	54.5	198.0	476.3
2001	-494.4	-82.9	233.4	35.4	198.0	485.4
2002	-304.0	8.7	-382.6	-95.6	-287.0	501.7
2003	-79.3	30.3	-546.3	-70.2	-476.4	529.4
2004	-67.9	136.8	-469.1	-33.0	-436.1	530.0
2005	-477.5	-27.6	-367.6	7.2	-374.8	696.7
2006	-558.4	-182.1	-254.4	10.0	-264.4	835.2
2007	-100.1	77.0	-390.3	-55.3	-355.0	772.5
2008	520.2	-94.7	-790.8	-107.5	-683.3	611.3

Source: Board of Governors of the Federal Reserve System, Flow of Funds Accounts of the United States, Flows and Outstandings Fourth Quarter 2008, March 13, 2009.

Foreign capital inflows augment domestic U.S. sources of capital, which, in turn, keep U.S. interest rates lower than they would be without the foreign capital. Indeed economists generally argue that it is this interplay between the demand for and the supply of credit in the economy that drives the broad inflows and outflows of capital. As U.S. demands for capital outstrip domestic sources of funds, domestic interest rates rise relative to those abroad, which tends to draw capital away from other countries to the United States. During periods of uncertainty, foreign investors often turn to U.S. Treasury securities as a "safe haven" investment, as was the case at times in 2008 and into 2009.

The United States also has benefitted from a surplus of saving over investment in many areas of the world that has provided a supply of funds and accommodated the overall shortfall of saving in the country. This surplus of saving has been available to the United States, because foreigners have remained willing to loan that saving to the United States in the form of acquiring U.S. assets, which have accommodated the growing current account deficits. Over the past decade, the United States experienced a decline in its rate of saving and an increase in the rate of domestic investment, as indicated in **Table 3**. The large increase in the nation's current account deficit would not have been possible without the accommodating inflows of foreign capital.

As **Table 3** indicates, compared with the 2002-2007 period, world saving in 2008 increased by 1.6% of gross domestic product (GDP), while investment increased by 1.3% of GDP. This shift toward greater saving relative to investment made it possible for the United states to invest more as a share of its GDP than its own saving could support through accommodating capital inflows. Among other advanced economies saving in 2008 fell relative to investment. In the emerging developing economies of Asia and the Middle East, saving increased faster than investment in 2008, which supplied the excess saving to the rest of the world. In the developing economies of Asia (which includes China), and the Middle East, saving as a share of GDP increased faster, and in some cases much faster, than did investment, which also increased in these areas.

Capital inflows also allow the United States to finance its trade deficit, because foreigners are willing to lend to the United States in the form of exchanging the sale of goods, represented by U.S. imports, for such U.S. assets as businesses and real estate (referred to as direct investment), and stocks, bonds, and U.S. Treasury securities. In 2008, the value of many of those assets dropped sharply, as the financial crisis eroded the value of financial assets and the economic downturn reduced profits and the value of on-going businesses. Such inflows, however, put upward pressure on the dollar, which tends to push up the price of U.S. exports relative to its imports and to reduce the overall level of exports. Furthermore, foreign investment in the U.S. economy drains off some of the income earned on the foreign-owned assets that otherwise would accrue to the U.S. economy as foreign investors repatriate their earnings back home.

Table 3. Saving and Investment in Selected Countries and Areas; 1994-2001, 2002-2007, and 2008 (Percentage of Gross Domestic Product)

Area/Country	Average, 1994-2001	Average, 2002-2007	2008	Change
World				
Saving	22.1	22.4	24.0	1.6
Investment	22.4	22.2	23.5	1.3
United States				
Saving	17.0	14.3	12.6	-1.7
Investment	19.6	19.2	17.5	-1.7
Other Advanced Economies				
Saving	21.6	19.9	19.6	-0.3
Investment	21.8	20.7	20.7	0.1
Eurozone				
Saving	21.4	21.5	21.8	0.3
Investment	21.0	20.8	22.2	1.4
Japan				
Saving	29.3	27.1	27.4	0.3
Investment	26.9	23.4	23.4	0.0
Newly Industrialized Asian Economies				
Saving	33.0	31.5	31.6	0.1
Investment	29.9	25.6	26.9	1.3
Emerging Developing Economies				
Saving	24.2	30.3	33.7	3.4
Investment	25.0	27.2	29.7	2.5
Developing Asia				
Saving	32.7	39.8	44.6	4.6
Investment	32.4	35.7	39.2	3.5
Middle East				
Saving	25.5	37.7	47.4	9.7
Investment	22.4	23.7	24.5	0.8

Source: *World Economic Outlook*, International Monetary Fund, October 2008. p. 286-289.

Some observers are particularly concerned about the long-term impact of the U.S. position as a net international investment debtor on the pattern of U.S. international income receipts and payments.[3] In 2007, the United States received $818 billion in income receipts on its investments abroad and paid out $736 billion in income payments on foreign-owned assets in the United States for a net surplus of $82 billion in income receipts, up from the $52 billion net surplus in income receipts experienced in 2006. Considering the overall negative balance of the U.S. net investment position, it is not surprising that the net surplus of income receipts is falling. As the annual amount of foreign investment in the U.S. economy continues to exceed the amount of U.S. investment abroad, however, it seems inevitable that U.S. payments on foreign-owned assets will continue to rise relative to U.S. receipts. A net outflow of income payments acts as a drag on the national economy as U.S. national income is reduced by the net amount of funds that are channeled abroad to foreign investors.

Foreign capital inflows, while important, do not fully replace or compensate for a lack of domestic sources of capital. Capital mobility has increased sharply over the last twenty years, but economic analysis shows that a nation's rate of capital formation, or domestic investment, seems to be linked primarily to its domestic rate of saving. This phenomenon was first presented in a paper published in 1980 by Martin Feldstein and Charles Horioka.[4] The Feldstein-Horioka paper maintained that despite the dramatic growth in capital flows between nations, international capital mobility remains somewhat limited so that a nation's rate of domestic investment is linked to its domestic rate of saving.[5]

Capital Flows and the Dollar

Another aspect of capital mobility and capital inflows is the impact such capital flows have on the international exchange value of the dollar. Demand for U.S. assets, such as financial securities, translates into demand for the dollar, since U.S. securities are denominated in dollars. As demand for the dollar rises or falls according to overall demand for dollar-denominated assets, the value of the dollar changes. These exchange rate changes, in turn, have secondary effects on the prices of U.S. and foreign goods, which tend to alter the U.S. trade balance. At times, foreign governments have moved aggressively in international capital markets to acquire the dollar directly or to acquire Treasury securities in order to strengthen the value of the dollar against particular currencies.

Also, the dollar is heavily traded in financial markets around the globe and, at times, plays the role of a global currency. Disruptions in this role have important implications for the United States and for the smooth functioning of the international financial system. This prominent role means that the exchange value of the dollar often acts as a mechanism for transmitting economic and political news and events across national borders. While such a role helps facilitate a broad range of international economic and financial activities, it also means that the dollar's exchange value can vary greatly on a daily or weekly basis as it is buffeted by international events.[6] A triennial survey of the world's leading central banks conducted by the Bank for International Settlements in April 2007 indicates that the **daily** trading of foreign currencies through traditional foreign exchange markets[7] totals more than $3.2 trillion, up sharply from the $1.9 trillion reported in the previous survey conducted in 2004, as indicated in **Table 4**. In addition to the traditional foreign exchange market, the over-the-counter (OTC)[8] foreign exchange derivatives market reported that daily turnover of interest rate and non-traditional foreign exchange derivatives contracts reached $2.1 trillion in April 2007. The combined amount of $5.3 trillion for daily foreign exchange trading in the traditional and OTC markets is more than three times the **annual** amount of U.S. exports of goods and services. The data also indicate that 86.3% of the global foreign exchange turnover is in U.S. dollars, slightly lower than the 88.7% share reported in a similar survey conducted in 2004.[9]

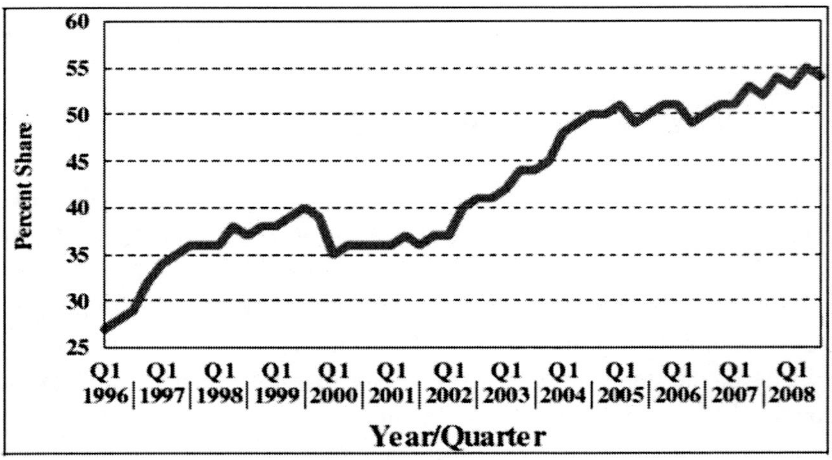

Source: *Treasury Bulletin*, U.S. Department of the Treasury

Figure 2. Foreign Ownership Share of Publicly Held Treasury Securities, 1996-2008

In the U.S. foreign exchange market, the value of the dollar is followed closely by multinational firms, international banks, and investors who are attempting to offset some of the inherent risks involved with foreign exchange trading. On a daily basis, turnover in the U.S. foreign exchange market[10] averages $664 billion; similar transactions in the U.S. foreign exchange derivative markets[11] averages $607 billion, nearly double the amount reported in a similar survey conducted in 2004.[12] Foreigners also buy and sell U.S. corporate bonds and stocks and U.S. Treasury securities. Foreigners now own about 53% of the total amount of outstanding U.S. Treasury securities that are publicly held and traded, as indicated in **Figure 2**.[13]

Table 4. Foreign Exchange Market Turnover Daily averages in April, in billions of U.S. dollars

	1992	1995	1998	2001	2004	2007
Foreign Exchange Market Turnover						
Instrument						
Spot transactions	$394	494	568	386	621	1,005
Outright forwards	58	97	128	130	208	362
Foreign exchange swaps	324	546	734	656	944	1,714
Reporting gaps	43	53	61	28	107	129
Total "traditional" turnover	820	1,190	1,490	1,200	1,880	3,210
Over the Counter Derivatives Market Turnover						
Foreign exchange instruments			97	87	140	291
Interest rate instruments			265	489	1,025	2,090
Reporting gaps			13	19	55	113
Total OTC turnover			375	575	1,220	2,090
Total market turnover	820	1,190	1,865	1,775	3,100	5,300
United States						
Foreign exchange turnover		244	351	254	461	664
OTC derivate-ives turnover			90	135	355	607
Total		244	441	389	816	1,271

Source: Triennial Central Bank Survey: Foreign Exchange and Derivatives Market Activity in 2007. Bank for International Settlement, September 2007.

PURCHASE AND SALES OF U.S. SECURITIES

A comprehensive set of data on capital flows, represented by purchases and sales of U.S. government securities and U.S. and foreign corporate stocks, bonds, into and out of the United States is published by the Treasury Department on a monthly basis.[14] These data represent crossborder flows and positions between U.S. residents and foreign residents and include monthly data on transactions in long-term securities, monthly and quarterly data on long- and short-term securities reported by banks and securities brokers, annual position data on holdings of long-term and short-term securities, and comprehensive benchmark surveys. Cross-border transactions consist of only those transactions that involve both a U.S. seller and a foreign purchaser; they exclude transactions between strictly U.S. buyers and sellers and foreign buyers and sellers. The data also capture only those transactions that involve a defined panel of custodians (banks and other depository institutions, securities brokers and dealers, end-investors, security issuers, and nonfinancial institutions) above a certain threshold amount, specifically cross-border transactions of at least $50 million per month. The custodial basis of the transactions means that some attribution of data to specific countries may distort the holdings data, because some foreign owners entrust the safekeeping of their securities to such financial centers as Belgium, the Caribbean banking centers, Luxembourg, Switzerland, and the United Kingdom, which would inflate the holdings of these custodians, rather than be attributed to the actual foreign owner. The data in the following tables reflect monthly transactions in long-term securities.[15]

As the data in **Table 5** show, foreign investors buy and sell large amounts of U.S. financial assets, although the annual accumulation, though large in dollar amounts, is relatively small compared with the large amounts of assets that are traded. For instance, in 2008 foreigners purchased $38 trillion dollars in U.S. financial assets and sold $37.8 trillion dollars in assets, for a net accumulation of $453 billion in financial assets, or less than 2% of the amount of assets that were traded.

Marketable U.S. Treasury securities generally account for one of the largest shares of U.S. securities that are traded by foreign investors, whether measured in terms of the total amount of securities that are bought and sold, or in terms of the net annual accumulation of financial assets. The low risk associated with these securities makes them highly desired, especially during periods of market uncertainty. In 2008, foreign trading in Treasury securities accounted for half of all the U.S. securities traded by foreign investors during the year, and the net amount of Treasury securities that were accumulated comprise the largest category of securities that were accumulated during the year, reflecting the impact the financial crisis and the economic recession had on foreign investor's appetite for other, more risky, types of investments, especially corporate stocks. Demand for Treasury securities often remains strong during uncertain times as a "safe haven" investment, including during the period following the terrorist attacks of September 11, 2001, when important elements of the U.S. financial system were temporarily shut down.[16]

Table 5. Transactions in Long-Term U.S. Securities, 2008 (in billions of dollars)

Total	Marketable Treasury Securities	U.S. Govt. Bonds	Corporate Bonds	Corporate Stocks	Foreign Bonds	Foreign Stocks
Gross Purchases by Foreigners						
$38,368.8	$14,627.5	$2,588.9	$1,467.1	$11,990.6	$2,263.6	$5,431.0
Gross Sales by Foreigners						
37,854.2	14,311.5	2,626.7	1,373.5	11,949.9	2,181.6	5,410.9
Net Purchases by Foreigners						
452.5	217.4	149.8	107.5	32.3	-14.1	-40.3

Source: Treasury Department International Capital data system, February 17, 2009.

Table 6 shows gross purchases, gross sales, and net sales of publicly traded long-term U.S. Treasury securities, corporate stocks, and corporate bonds over the seven-year period 2001 to 2007. At over $15 trillion, Treasury securities were the most heavily traded of the three kinds of securities in 2007. From 1997 to 2001, foreign official and private net acquisitions of Treasury securities plummeted as the Federal government used its budget surpluses to retire large amounts of securities, as indicated in **Figure 3**. The Federal government's budget deficits from 2002 through 2007, however, provided new opportunities for foreign investors to build up their holdings of Treasury securities.

As **Figure 3** indicates, foreign private purchases of Treasury securities turned negative between 1998 and 2001 and again in 2006 as foreign private investors experienced net sales of Treasury securities. From 2002 to 2006 and again in 2007, foreign private investors returned to acquiring Treasury securities, but the amount they acquired remained relatively level at $100 billion per year. In contrast, foreign official net acquisitions of Treasury securities trended slightly upward between 2000 and 2002, but such net acquisitions more than doubled over the 2002 to 2004 period, rising to $261 billion in 2004. In 2005, though, official purchases of Treasury securities plummeted to less than $100 billion and were less than private purchases. In 2006, private foreign investors again reduced their net holdings of Treasury securities. This action was offset by a large increase in acquisitions of Treasury securities by foreign governments, directed at least in part to slow the decline in the international exchange value of the dollar. In 2007, foreign private investors returned to acquiring treasury securities, with a net accumulation of $116 billion, while net foreign official purchases dropped to about $60 billion.

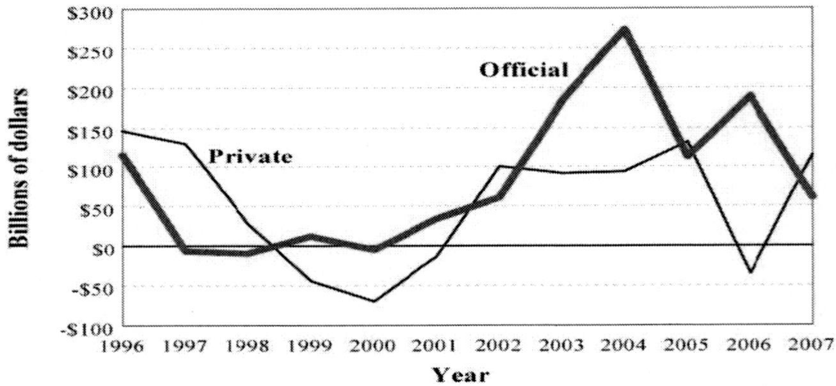

Source: Department of Commerce

Figure 3. Foreign Official and Private Purchases of U.S. Treasury Securities, 1996-2007

While the nominal amount of total purchases and sales of corporate bonds on an annual basis has been much lower than that for Treasury securities, the strong net accumulation of corporate bonds surpassed that of Treasury securities in 2007. This attraction to corporate bonds likely reflects the attractiveness of bonds to foreign investors as an alternative to Treasury securities and as a hedge against falling interest rates. The price of a bond is inversely related to the interest rate, so lowering interest rates raises the price of a bond and makes the bond more valuable. Net accumulations of corporate stocks has been the most volatile of the three groups of securities over the decade. High levels of stock accumulation at the beginning and end of the period may well reflect low levels of accumulation of Treasury securities and a rise in stocks prices that marked those periods. Economic uncertainties and lower rates of national economic growth, however, characterized the years during the middle part of the period.

Table 6. Foreign Transactions in U.S. Securities, 2002-2008 (in billions of dollars)

	2002	2003	2004	2005	2006	2007	2008
Treasury Securities							
Purchases	$7,264.5	$8,001.5	$8,936.0	$10,051.2	$10,957.9	$15,127.5	$14,627.5
Sales	7,144.5	7,737.9	8,584.0	9,713.1	10,762.4	14,929.6	14,311.5
Net	119.9	263.6	352.1	338.1	195.5	198.0	316.0
Corporate Stocks							
Purchases	3,209.8	3,104.2	3,862.0	4,731.7	6,868.6	10,639.7	11,990.6
Sales	3,159.6	3,069.5	3,833.6	4,649.8	6,718.2	10,443.8	11,949.9
Net	50.2	34.7	28.5	82.0	150.4	195.5	40.8
Corporate Bonds							
Purchases	820.7	979.9	1,171.4	1,277.0	1,678.5	1,913.3	1,467.1
Sales	638.4	714.2	861.9	904.8	1,167.7	1,520.0	1,373.5
Net	182.3	265.7	309.5	372.2	510.8	393.4	93.5

Source: Treasury Department International Capital data system, February 17, 2009.

Table 7. Net Foreign Purchases of U.S. Securities by Foreigners (in billions of dollars)

	2002	2003	2004	2005	2006	2007	2008	Total
Total ($)	574.6	663.3	763.6	839.1	892.3	776.6	514.6	5,024.1
Total Europe	258.3	279.6	239.4	428.8	378.1	328.3	272.0	2,184.5
-France	2.4	-0.4	-9.1	19.7	36.2	9.0	4.8	62.7
-Germany	0.0	12.5	16.8	23.8	-5.3	8.8	-1.2	55.4
-Italy	2.3	-2.4	-2.1	1.0	-3.2	-1.1	5.8	0.3
-Netherlands	-8.6	3.6	0.5	-6.7	4.2	14.0	-3.7	3.2
-Sweden	4.9	2.9	-3.5	-9.5	5.7	7.1	17.7	25.4
-Switzerland	8.6	13.0	13.7	-4.7	7.7	-8.9	14.6	44.1
-United Kingdom	191.9	159.8	142.6	317.2	314.7	391.7	330.5	1,848.3
Canada	6.8	32.4	24.0	48.2	25.4	10.4	17.2	164.5
Latin America	92.2	108.5	149.4	146.1	217.2	156.8	-51.2	818.9
-Mexico	10.2	10.8	28.2	18.9	14.6	8.3	12.3	103.2
Asia	203.4	234.4	364.7	221.5	266.3	261.5	326.2	1,878.0
-China	62.9	68.9	49.4	89.2	117.3	122.5	142.4	652.5
-Hong Kong	14.6	16.4	22.2	33.6	42.9	90.4	78.7	298.7
-Indonesia	1.4	1.6	2.8	-1.4	1.7	2.7	-6.2	2.5
-Japan	81.4	137.1	226.5	47.0	60.2	3.7	74.1	629.9
-Korea	13.0	12.2	15.7	6.1	14.5	6.2	-18.0	49.7
-Malaysia	0.9	-1.4	-0.7	4.5	-0.0	5.1	3.3	11.7
-Philippines	-1.0	0.3	-0.6	1.2	-0.7	4.8	-1.7	2.4
-Singapore	12.0	8.7	17.0	13.2	-1.5	10.2	7.6	67.1
-Taiwan	17.4	-1.9	10.7	10.7	4.9	8.0	11.8	61.7
-Thailand	-1.4	-5.6	-0.2	7.7	0.8	1.9	-1.4	1.8
-Australia	10.2	4.3	-8.5	-6.9	-2.5	6.1	-14.2	-11.5

Source: Developed by CRS from the Treasury Department's International Capital data system. February 17, 2009.

PURCHASES AND SALES OF U.S. SECURITIES BY FOREIGN INVESTORS

Some foreign investors are more active in U.S. securities markets—U.S. Treasury securities, U.S. corporate stocks and bonds—than are others. Over the period from 2002 to 2008, foreign investors are estimated to have accumulated over $5 trillion in U.S. securities. As **Table 7** indicates, the United Kingdom is estimated to have accumulated $1.8 trillion U.S. securities over the 2002-2008 period.

A large accumulation by British investors is not surprising given the long historical involvement of British investors in the U.S. economy. Other foreign investors have started acquiring U.S. securities more recently. Some, such as Chinese investors, have moved rapidly to become major investors in some U.S. securities markets. British investors are followed by Chinese investors as the second largest foreign investors with $652 billion in U.S. securities during the 2002-2008 period, or about one-third the amount owned by British investors. During the seven year period, Japanese investors were the third most active investors in U.S. securities, with $630 billion in securities holdings. Following Japan, Hong Kong ($299 billion), Canada ($164), Mexico ($103 billion), Singapore ($67 billion), Germany ($63 billion), and Taiwan ($62 billion) accumulated the largest amounts of U.S. securities over the 2002-2008 period.

Treasury Securities

As previously indicated, foreign investors are active participates in the U.S. Treasury securities market. Over the seven-year period of 2002-2008, foreign investors acquired on net (purchases less sales) about $1.8 trillion dollars in Treasury securities, as indicated in **Table 8**. The United Kingdom acquired an estimated $800 billion in U.S. publicly held and traded Treasury securities over the 2002-2008 period, followed by Japan, which accumulated $297 billion during the period. China, a recent participant in the U.S. Treasury securities market accumulated the third largest amount of these securities with $228 billion in holdings. Nearly half of China's holdings were acquired during 2005 and 2007. Canada ($64 billion) accumulated the next largest amount of Treasury securities, followed by Hong Kong ($35 billion).

Table 8. Net Foreign Purchases of Publicly Traded U.S. Treasury Securities (in billions of dollars)

	2002	2003	2004	2005	2006	2007	2008	Total
Total	$119.9	$263.6	$352.1	$338.1	$195.5	$198.0	$316.0	$1,783.2
Total Europe	43.7	48.7	88.4	173.6	99.0	177.3	196.6	827.3
-France	-0.3	-7.0	-10.2	9.6	-1.6	-7.8	-15.4	-32.8
-Germany	-3.9	11.0	8.8	14.5	2.1	-3.5	0.7	29.8
-Italy	-0.3	-2.9	0.0	3.8	0.2	-1.5	0.8	0.1
-Netherlands	-17.0	0.4	-3.2	-6.1	0.7	1.5	-4.8	-28.5
-Sweden	2.9	0.4	3.2	1.8	0.7	2.2	-3.1	8.2
-Switzerland	-0.4	4.9	5.3	-4.9	-2.9	-2.6	1.2	0.5
-United Kingdom	61.6	32.8	78.7	134.1	91.8	208.6	188.6	796.2
Canada	-5.2	10.4	16.1	21.5	14.2	-1.9	9.1	64.1
Latin America	20.0	17.1	33.5	68.4	12.0	88.5	23.2	262.8
-Mexico	4.0	5.3	8.4	9.8	-0.3	1.5	-7.1	21.5
Asia	55.7	181.1	214.8	68.3	68.7	-69.3	98.9	618.2
-China	24.1	30.4	18.9	37.4	40.6	-8.0	84.7	228.2
-Hong Kong	-9.1	6.1	1.1	12.3	16.3	2.0	6.2	35.0
-Indonesia	0.8	0.7	1.2	1.2	2.1	4.5	-5.9	4.6
-Japan	30.5	146.5	166.4	-5.0	1.3	-48.7	6.1	297.1
-Korea	12.9	4.5	5.9	1.5	6.2	-17.9	-11.2	1.8
-Malaysia	0.9	-0.3	0.4	1.1	-2.4	0.4	-0.9	-0.9
-Philippines	0.2	0.4	0.1	1.1	-0.2	3.1	-2.1	2.6
-Singapore	-2.6	-1.4	3.5	2.4	-2.2	2.5	-7.0	-4.9
-Thailand	-1.9	-6.1	-0.4	8.4	1.3	0.8	-2.9	-0.8
-Australia	3.3	6.6	-2.2	0.1	-2.6	-1.4	-3.0	0.9

Source: Developed by CRS from the Treasury Department's International Capital data system, February 17, 2009.

Corporate Stocks

Net foreign acquisitions of U.S. corporate stocks fell sharply in 2008, after reached a record high in 2007, as foreign investors acquired $41 billion in corporate stocks, as indicated in **Table 9**. This amount was the lowest amount of net acquisitions since 2004 and accounts for just onefourth the amount of stocks acquired in 2007. In total, foreign investors accumulated $582 billion in U.S. corporate stocks in the 2002-2008 period, most of which was acquired in the 2006-2007 period. British investors are by far the largest investors in U.S. corporate stocks, with estimated holdings acquired over the 2002-2008 period totaling $226 billion, reflecting the interdependence between the U.S. and

U.K. financial markets.. Over the 2002-2008 period, Canada and France were the next two largest foreign acquirers of U.S. corporate stocks with such investments estimated to total $69 billion and $62 billion, respectively. Hong Kong ($39 billion), Singapore ($23 billion) and the Netherlands ($16 billion), followed by Japan ($14 billion) and Switzerland ($10 billion) are the next largest foreign investors in U.S. corporate stocks.

Table 9. Net Foreign Purchases of U.S. Corporate Stocks (in billions of dollars)

	2002	2003	2004	2005	2006	2007	2008	Total
Total	$50.2	$34.7	$28.5	$82.0	$150.4	195.5	40.8	582.0
Total Europe	32.9	21.4	19.6	39.6	97.1	89.3	11.6	311.4
-France	2.1	6.2	-0.9	7.7	21.7	19.5	-7.2	49.2
-Germany	-0.1	-3.8	-2.4	-3.3	-8.0	0.6	-19.3	-36.3
-Italy	1.5	0.4	-1.7	-2.6	-2.3	-4.3	-1.8	-10.8
-Netherlands	4.3	0.0	1.7	-2.3	-5.4	6.9	-1.5	3.8
-Sweden	0.8	3.4	0.8	-0.5	0.7	0.3	5.1	10.5
-Switzerland	2.8	-2.1	-1.2	1.3	1.2	-3.0	5.4	4.4
-United Kingdom	15.2	0.7	15.2	19.8	75.8	69.5	29.9	226.0
Canada	8.2	11.7	1.3	16.5	11.8	8.1	7.4	65.0
Latin America	-15.4	-0.9	0.6	15.3	37.2	49.4	-35.0	51.2
-Mexico	0.5	-0.3	-0.2	-0.3	1.8	0.1	0.5	2.1
Asia	21.4	2.8	6.2	10.2	3.5	44.0	65.3	153.3
-China	0.2	-0.1	-0.3	-0.5	0.5	4.0	-0.7	3.0
-Hong Kong	1.8	0.8	-0.8	1.1	-0.5	35.4	27.5	65.3
-Indonesia	-0.0	0.1	0.0	-0.1	-0.0	-0.1	-0.0	-0.1
-Japan	12.3	-2.2	2.8	0.1	-0.7	-5.0	21.4	28.8
-Korea	0.1	-0.0	-0.0	-0.1	-0.1	0.1	2.8	2.7
-Malaysia	-0.0	-0.0	-0.1	-0.2	-0.0	0.3	0.0	0.0
-Philippines	-0.0	-0.0	0.0	0.1	0.0	0.0	-0.0	0.1
-Singapore	8.2	3.5	-1.7	7.2	-4.5	-2.5	4.7	14.9
-Thailand	0.0	-0.0	0.0	-0.0	-0.0	-0.0	0.0	-0.1
-Australia	3.0	-0.6	0.3	0.1	1.0	4.8	0.3	9.0

Source: Developed by CRS from the Treasury Department's International Capital data system. February 17, 2009.

Corporate Bonds

As **Table 10** indicates, foreign investors have shown particular interest in U.S. corporate bonds over the 2001-2007 period and accumulated about $2.2

trillion in such securities during the seven-year period. A large share of these accumulations is concentrated among a few large holders. For instance, British investors hold nearly half of the foreign-owned U.S. corporate bonds, with an estimated accumulation of $1.0 trillion over the 2001-2007 period. Japanese investors trail behind their British counterparts, but acquired an estimated $138 billion in corporate bonds in the 2001-2007 period. China ($129 billion), France ($57 billion), Hong Kong ($57 billion), Switzerland ($34 billion), and Singapore ($28 billion), and are estimated to be the next largest foreign investors in U.S. corporate bonds during the 2001-2007 period. Latin American and Caribbean countries acquired $420 billion in U.S. corporate bonds over the 2001-2007 period, slightly greater than the $409 billion acquired by countries in Asia.

Table 10. Net Foreign Purchases of U.S. Corporate Bonds (in billions of dollars)

	2002	2003	2004	2005	2006	2007	2008	Total
Total	$182.3	$265.7	$309.5	$372.2	$510.8	$393.4	$93.5	$2,127.5
Total Europe	110.7	169.2	172.0	241.7	316.1	207.5	-5.8	1,211.5
-France	2.6	4.0	7.6	13.2	22.1	4.3	-2.0	51.8
-Germany	2.0	3.5	12.2	6.5	-11.8	5.4	5.0	22.7
-Italy	0.2	2.0	0.7	-0.1	-0.5	-0.1	0.2	2.4
-Netherlands	1.5	2.3	2.1	2.8	3.2	-0.7	-0.4	10.8
-Sweden	0.2	0.2	1.1	-0.4	2.2	1.7	-0.5	4.5
-Switzerland	4.9	5.7	4.0	3.7	9.7	3.6	11.9	43.6
-United Kingdom	76.8	107.7	107.1	168.9	253.8	209.0	31.9	955.1
Canada	0.4	5.3	6.1	2.2	8.1	12.3	7.2	41.6
Latin America	40.9	61.1	67.8	47.7	101.3	46.8	26.3	392.0
-Mexico	2.2	3.0	15.1	1.6	3.9	1.9	1.7	29.3
Asia	26.4	27.8	60.1	70.9	76.9	120.0	64.6	446.9
-China	6.0	4.8	12.3	26.1	31.2	41.7	29.6	151.6
-Hong Kong	3.7	4.5	5.7	11.0	14.8	12.8	7.0	59.6
-Indonesia	0.1	0.0	-0.1	0.0	0.2	0.4	0.0	0.7
-Japan	10.9	10.6	33.5	25.6	12.6	39.6	22.3	155.0
-Korea	1.5	0.5	1.6	0.8	3.2	11.3	0.6	19.5
-Malaysia	0.1	0.0	0.1	1.3	1.1	2.1	0.3	5.0
-Philippines	0.1	0.1	0.2	0.1	0.2	0.2	0.1	0.9
-Singapore	1.3	3.0	4.2	1.0	6.0	6.9	-1.1	21.4
-Thailand	0.2	0.4	0.1	-0.0	0.1	0.0	0.2	1.0
-Australia	3.0	0.4	1.4	6.3	7.2	5.0	0.3	23.7

Source: Developed by CRS from the Treasury Department's International Capital data system, February 17, 2009.

Major Foreign Holdings of U.S. Long-Term Securities

As **Table 11** indicates, total foreign holdings, or the cumulative amount, of marketable and nonmarketable U.S. Treasury bills, bonds, and notes amounted to over $2.4 trillion at year-end 2007. These holdings are divided into foreign private holdings designated by the individual country data and holdings by foreign official institutions, which amounted to $1.5 trillion in 2007, or more than the $882 billion accumulated by private investors. The data for foreign official institutions consist of more than the foreign reserve asset holdings of central banks and of other foreign government institutions involved in the formulation of international monetary policy. These holdings also include the holdings of foreign government-sponsored investment funds and other foreign government investment funds. Distinguishing between foreign private and official holdings, however, can be difficult, because chains of intermediaries can obscure the country and the type of foreign holder. As a result, foreign official holdings likely are undercounted in these data.

With $571 billion in long-term Treasury securities holdings accumulated over the 2001-2007 period, Japan is the single largest holder of such securities. Over the same period, China had accumulated $406 billion in such holdings by 2007. Between 2001 and 2007, China increased its holdings of Treasury securities by more than five times. With $300 billion, the United Kingdom ranked third in holdings behind China and held more than the $127 billion accumulated by the oil exporting countries.[17]

Table 12 shows the relative shares of foreign holdings of total U.S. securities from 1974 to 2000. These data indicate that between 1974 and 1984, there was little growth in the relative shares of foreign holdings of various types of U.S. long-term securities. Since 1984, however, there has been significant growth in the foreign share of all types of long-term securities, particularly in the foreign share of long-term marketable U.S. Treasury securities, which grew from 13% of the total amount outstanding to in 1984 to 35% of the total in 2000. In total, foreign investors hold 10% of the combined value of outstanding U.S. corporate equity, corporate and municipal bonds, marketable Treasury securities, and other U.S. government securities.

Table 11. Major Foreign Holdings of Long-Term U.S. Treasury Securities, or Cumulative Amounts (in billions of dollars)

Country	2008	2007	2006	2005	2004	2003	2002
China	$727.4	$477.6	$396.9	$310.0	$222.9	$159.0	$118.4
Japan	626.0	579.9	622.9	670.0	689.9	550.8	378.1
Carib Banking Centers	197.5	117.4	72.3	77.2	51.1	47.3	50.3
Oil Exporters	186.2	137.9	110.2	78.2	62.1	42.6	49.6
United Kingdom	130.9	157.9	92.6	146.0	95.8	82.2	80.8
Brazil	127.0	129.9	52.1	28.7	15.2	11.8	12.7
Russia	116.4	32.7	7.0	N.A.	N.A.	N.A.	N.A.
Luxembourg	97.4	69.0	60.0	35.6	41.4	25.4	23.9
Hong Kong	77.2	51.1	54.0	40.3	45.1	50.0	47.5
Taiwan	71.8	38.2	59.4	68.1	67.9	50.9	37.4
Switzerland	62.3	38.9	34.3	30.8	41.7	46.1	34.0
Germany	56.1	41.3	46.0	49.9	50.3	47.8	37.3
Ireland	54.3	18.7	11.6	19.7	16.2	14.9	7.0
Singapore	40.8	39.8	31.3	33.0	30.4	21.2	17.8
Mexico	34.8	34.2	34.9	35.0	32.8	27.4	24.9
Thailand	32.4	27.4	16.9	16.1	12.5	11.7	17.2
Korea	31.3	39.2	66.7	69.0	55.0	63.1	38.0
Turkey	30.8	25.6	23.0	17.4	12.0	15.7	13.5
India	29.2	14.9	14.6	N.A.	15.0	16.7	9.2
Norway	23.1	26.2	N.A.	N.A.	22.6	5.2	N.A.
Israel	18.8	5.6	15.6	12.5	13.7	12.2	12.5
Egypt	17.2	10.4	N.A.	N.A.	N.A.	N.A.	N.A.
France	16.8	9.8	26.4	30.9	20.1	17.2	22.9
Italy	16.0	14.6	13.2	15.4	12.9	13.2	16.3
Belgium	15.9	13.2	16.3	17.0	17.0	14.4	13.0
Netherlands	15.4	15.2	20.7	15.7	16.0	12.3	13.0
Chile	15.2	8.7	N.A.	N.A.	N.A.	N.A.	N.A.
Sweden	12.7	13.7	12.0	16.3	17.0	9.9	12.3
Philippines	11.7	10.1	N.A.	N.A.	N.A.	N.A.	N.A.
Columbia	11.1	7.3	N.A.	N.A.	N.A.	N.A.	N.A.
All Other	173.1	144.6	148.0	159.4	128.9	119.2	110.1
Grand Total	3,076.9	2,351.1	2,103.0	2,033.9	1,849.3	1,523.1	1,235.6
Foreign Official	2,138.7	1,643.2	1,449.0	1,279.9	1,233.3	933.9	760.1
Treasury Bills	457.9	198.4	176.8	201.9	245.2	212.0	190.4
T-Bonds & Notes	1,680.8	1,444.8	1,272.0	1,078.1	988.1	721.9	569.7

Source: U.S. Department of the Treasury. Data represent estimated foreign holdings of U.S. Treasury marketable and non-marketable bills, bonds, and notes. Data represent totals as of the end of December of the year indicated.

Table 12. Market Value of Foreign Holdings of U.S. Long-Term Securities, by Type of Security (in billions of dollars)

	Total outstanding	Foreign owned	Percent foreign owned
Corporate equity			
1974	$663	$25	3.8%
1978	1,012	48	4.7%
1984	1,899	105	5.5%
1989	4,212	275	6.5%
1994	7,183	398	5.5%
2000	23,038	1,711	7.4%
Corporate and municipal debts			
1974	458	N.A.	N.A.
1978	680	7	1.0%
1984	1,149	31	2.7%
1989	2,400	190	7.9%
1994	3,342	276	8.3%
2000	5,404	712	13.2%
Marketable U.S. Treasury securities			
1974	163	24	14.7%
1978	326	39	12.0%
1984	873	118	13.5%
1989	1,599	333	20.8%
1994	2,392	464	19.4%
2000	2,508	885	35.3%
U.S. government corporation and federally sponsored agency securities			
1974	106	N.A.	N.A.
1978	188	5	2.7%
1984	529	13	2.5%
1989	1,267	48	3.8%
1994	2,199	107	4.9%
2000	3,968	257	6.4%
Combined market			
1974	1,390	67	4.8%
1978	2,206	99	4.5%
1984	4,450	268	6.0%
1989	9,478	847	8.9%
1994	15,116	1,244	8.2%
2000	34,918	3,576	10.2%

Source: Griever, William L., Gary A. Lee, and Francis E. Warnock, The U.S. System for Measuring Cross-Border Investment in Securities: A Primer with a Discussion of Recent Developments. *Federal Reserve Bulletin*, October 2001. 639.

ECONOMIC IMPLICATIONS

The large foreign accumulation of U.S. securities, particularly of U.S. Treasury securities, has spurred some observers to consider the potential for a financial crisis. Such a crisis could result from a coordinated withdrawal from U.S. financial markets staged by foreign investors for economic or political reasons or a sharp drop in U.S. equity prices as a result of an uncoordinated correction in market prices.[18] Congress likely would find itself embroiled in any such crisis through its direct role in conducting fiscal policy and in its indirect role in the conduct of monetary policy through its supervisory responsibility over the Federal Reserve. A coordinated withdrawal from U.S. securities markets by foreign investors seems highly unlikely, particularly since the vast majority of the investors are private entities that presumably would find it difficult to coordinate a withdrawal.

It is uncertain what events could provoke a coordinated withdrawal from U.S. securities markets. Some surmise that international concern over the ability of the economy to service its large foreign debt could spur foreign investors to rein in their purchases of U.S. financial assets, or that a loss of confidence in the ability of national U.S. policymakers to conduct economic policies that are perceived abroad as prudent and stabilizing could cause foreign investors to reassess their estimates of the risks involved in holding dollar-denominated assets. In other cases, the international linkages that connect national capital markets could be the conduit through which events in one market are quickly spread to other markets and ignite an abrupt, seemingly uncoordinated decline in equity prices. Such a market correction, or a market panic, is expected to be short-lived, however, as investors would likely move to take advantage of a drop in equityprices to acquire equities that would be deemed to be temporarily undervalued. For instance, concerns in U.S. capital markets in early June 2006 over prospects that a rise in consumer prices and in the core inflation rate would push the Federal Reserve to raise key U.S. interest rates sparked a drop in prices in U.S. capital and equity markets where inflation concerns quickly spread to markets in Europe and Asia, where equity prices fell as well.[19]

Short of a financial crisis, foreign capital inflows are playing an important role in the economy. Such inflows bridge the gap between U.S. supplies and demands for credit, thereby allowing the consumers and businesses to finance purchases at interest rates that are lower than they would be without the capital inflows. Similarly, capital inflows allow federal, state, and local governments to finance their budget deficits at rates that are lower then they would be otherwise.

Capital inflows, however, are not without some cost to the economy. Foreign ownership of U.S. securities means that foreigners receive any dividend or interest payments that arise from those securities and that the economy experiences a transfer of wealth associated with flows of goods and capital across borders. To the extent that foreign investors repatriate their earnings, financial resources within the economy are reduced. Increased foreign ownership of corporate stocks and bonds also blurs the distinction between domestic and foreign-owned firms and may well influence the way firms view trade, economic, and other types of public policies, thereby affecting their relationships with Congress. In addition, as long as credit demands in the economy outstrip domestic supplies of credit, foreign sources of capital will be necessary to reduce pressure on U.S. interest rates. To the extent that foreign investors become reluctant for any reason to continue to supply the economy with capital, Congress could find it more difficult to finance a budget deficit by drawing on domestic capital markets without the economy feeling the impact of such borrowing.

The prospect of continued high levels of U.S. borrowing from the rest of the world concerns various international organizations, such as the International Monetary Fund (IMF) and the Organization for Economic Cooperation and Development (OECD). In its April 2006 edition of *World Economic Outlook*,[20] the IMF highlighted the role U.S. economic policies played in the short run in stemming a potentially serious economic slowdown in both the United States and the global economy. Over the long run, however, the IMF argues that the saving-investment imbalance in the U.S. economy threatens to affect global interest rates, productivity and income, and the growing deficits in the nation's already large current account (exports, imports, and official capital flows) as a result of sustained high levels of capital inflows. These effects could be especially serious for many of the developing nations that rely on borrowing in global financial markets. Rising interest rates in the United States could raise interest rates globally, which would raise borrowing costs to developing countries. The IMF argues that, "over time changes in U.S. interest rates feed through about one-to-one to foreign interest rates, implying that, in the long run, the rest of the world is affected in a similar manner to the United States."[21]

In a May 2004 publication,[22] the OECD also questioned the feasibility of sustaining large trade deficits given that the deficits are accommodated by foreign investors who must remain willing to hold dollar-denominated assets.

Foreign investors essentially engage in cross-border risk management and will assess their estimates of risk based on a broad range of factors, including the ability of the economy to support a potentially increasing level of debt. According to the OECD, "While the United States remains an attractive investment destination in many respects, it is uncertain for how long foreigners will continue to accommodate debt and equity claims against U.S. residents at the recent pace."[23]

The highly evolved state of financial and economic linkages between the United States and other foreign economies significantly reduces the prospects of a financial collapse in the United States should foreigners attempt a coordinated withdrawal from U.S. securities markets. A withdrawal by any single large foreign investor, or a group of investors, from the U.S. financial markets at a time when those funds are necessary for closing the gap between domestic demand and supply of funds would likely have significant short-run effects. Any such coordinated attempt to withdraw substantial amounts of funds abruptly from the U.S. markets would ordinarily be noticed quickly by domestic and international financial markets. As investors became aware of any large withdrawals, they likely would follow suit, driving the prices of the asset down sharply and causing U.S. interest rates to rise abruptly. Any investor selling assets at this point likely would experience a significant loss in the value of those assets.

A similar downward spiral would occur over the short-run in the value of the dollar if foreign investors attempted to convert their dollar holdings into foreign currency. The financial and currency markets likely would adjust quickly to the demands of foreign sellers of dollars by driving up the price of foreign currencies. This likely would result in a decline in the value of the dollar and a further erosion in the value of the assets of foreigners attempting to withdraw from the U.S. markets.

Over the long run, the economic and financial effects of a foreign withdrawal from U.S. financial markets would be limited because those factors which allowed foreigners to withdraw would attract other foreign investors to the U.S. markets. As U.S. interest rates rose in response to the selling of securities, other investors likely would be attracted to the higher returns of the assets, which would curb the decline in the prices in the securities. Also, the rise in U.S. interest rates would attract foreign capital, which would limit the rise in interest rates. A decline in the value of the dollar against other currencies would also improve the international price competitiveness of U.S. goods. As a result, U.S. exports would increase, likely narrowing the gap between the earnings on U.S. exports and the amount Americans spend on imports, thereby reducing the amount of foreign capital the U.S. economy would need. Furthermore, those foreign investors who are successful in withdrawing their funds from the U.S. markets would have to find suitable alternatives. Even if they did not reinvest their finds in the United States, the infusion of capital back into foreign capital markets likely would have spillover effects on the United States and on U.S. securities.

It also seems unlikely that the Federal Reserve would sit on the sidelines watching while the U.S. economy suffered a financial collapse. In the immediate aftermath of the September 11, 2001 terrorist attacks, the U.S. financial and foreign exchange market activities were slightly out of the norm, but actions by the Federal Reserve and by other central banks helped head off a financial panic and a loss of confidence by ensuring that the financial system was supplied with liquidity through coordinated actions. Central bank coordination in times of crises is not uncommon, but the speed with which the coordination was reached and the aggressiveness of the banks to stem any loss of confidence in the financial system demonstrate the recognition that national economies have become highly interconnected and that a shock to one can create spillover effects onto other economies and markets.[24]

ENDNOTES

[1] Teplin, Albert M., the U.S. Flows of Funds Accounts and Their Uses, *Federal Reserve Bulletin*, July 2001. p. 431-441.

[2] Board of Governors of the Federal Reserve System, *Flow of Funds Accounts of the United States, Flows and Outstandings*, various issues.

[3] CRS Report RL32964, *The United States as a Net Debtor Nation: Overview of the International Investment Position*, by James K. Jackson.

[4] Feldstein, Martin, and Charles Horioka, Domestic Saving and International Capital Flows, *The Economic Journal*, June, 1980, pp. 314-329; Feldstein, Martin, *Aspects of Global Economic Integration: Outlook for the Future*. NBER Working Paper 7899, September 2000, pp. 9-12.

[5] Developments in capital markets have improved capital mobility since the Feldstein-Horioka paper was published and have led some economists to question Feldstein and Horioka's conclusion concerning the lack of perfect capital mobility. (Ghosh, Atish R., International Capital Mobility Amongst the Major Industrialized Countries: Too Little or Too Much?, *The Economic Journal*, January 1995, pp. 107-128.) Indeed, some authors argue that short-term capital flows among the major developed economies are highly liquid, perhaps too liquid, and seem to be driven as much by short-term economic events and speculation as they are by longer term economic trends.

[6] Samuelson, Robert J., Dangers in a Dollar on the Edge. *The Washington Post*, December 8, 2006. p. A39.

[7] Traditional foreign exchange markets are organized exchanges which trade primarily in foreign exchange futures and options contracts where the terms and condition of the contracts are standardized.

[8] The over-the-counter foreign exchange derivatives market is an informal market consisting of dealers who customtailor agreements to meet the specific needs regarding maturity, payments intervals or other terms that allow the contracts to meet specific requirements for risk.

[9] *Triennial Central Bank Survey: Foreign Exchange and Derivatives Market Activity in 2007.* Bank for International Settlement, September 2007. pp. 1-2. A copy of the report is available at:http://www.bis.org/publ/rpfx07.pdf

[10] Defined as foreign exchange transactions in the spot and forward exchange markets and foreign exchange swaps. A spot transaction is defined as a single transaction involving the exchange of two currencies at a rate agreed upon on the date of the contract; a foreign exchange swap is a multi-part transaction which involves the exchange of two currencies on a specified date at a rate agreed upon at the time of the conclusion of the contract and then a reverse exchange of the same two currencies at a date further in the future at a rate generally different from the rate applied to the first transaction.

[11] Defined as transactions in foreign reserve accounts, interest rate swaps, cross currency interest rate swaps, and foreign exchange and interest rate options. A currency swap commits two counterparties to exchange streams of interest payments in different currencies for an agreed upon period of time and usually to exchange principal amounts in different currencies as a pre-agreed exchange rate; a currency option conveys the right to buy or sell a currency with another currency as a specified rate during a specified period.

[12] *The Foreign Exchange and Interest Rate Derivatives Markets: Turnover in the United States April 2007.* The Federal Reserve Bank of New York, April, 2004. pp. 1-2. A copy of the report is available at http://www.newyorkfed.org/ markets/triennial/fx_survey.pdf.

[13] *Treasury Bulletin*, December 2007. Table OFS-2. p. 48.

[14] These data are available through the World Wide Web at Treasury Department's Treasury International Capital (TIC) reporting site: http://www.treas.gov/tic/.

[15] Bertaut, Carol C., William L. Griever, and Ralph W. Tryon, Understanding U.S. Cross-Border Securities Data, Federal Reserve Bulletin, 2006. p. A59-A75.

[16] For additional information, see CRS Report RS21102, *International Capital Flows Following the September 11 Attacks*, by James K. Jackson.

[17] Oil exporters include Ecuador, Venezuela, Indonesia, Bahrain, Iran, Iraq, Kuwait, Oman, Qatar,Saudi Arabia, the United Arab Emirates, Algeria, Gabon, Libya, and Nigeria.

[18] For a longer presentation of this topic, see CRS Report RL34319, *Foreign Ownership of U.S. Financial Assets:Implications of a Withdrawal*, by James K. Jackson.

[19] Masters, Brooke A., Pondering the Bear Necessities, *The Washington Post*, June 7, 2006, p. D1; Samuelson, Robert J., Global Capital On the Run, *The Washington Post*, June 14, 2006, p. A23.

[20] *World Economic Outlook*, International Monetary Fund. Washington, DC, April 2006.

[21] *World Economic Outlook*, International Monetary Fund. Washington, DC, April 2004. pp. 69-70.

[22] The Challenges of Narrowing the U.S. Current Account Deficit. *OECD Economic Outlook* No. 75, May 2004. Available at http://www.oecd.org/dataoecd/4/58/31920358.pdf.

[23] Ibid., p. 31.

[24] Jackson, International Capital Flows Following the September 11 Attacks.

In: Foreign Investment In U.S. Securities
Editors: Declan J. Byrne
ISBN: 978-1-60876-084-8

Chapter 4

FOREIGN OWNERSHIP OF U.S. FINANCIAL ASSETS: IMPLICATIONS OF A WITHDRAWAL

James K. Jackson

SUMMARY

This report provides an overview of the role foreign investment plays in the U.S. economy and an assessment of possible actions a foreign investor or a group of foreign investors might choose to take to liquidate their investments in the United States. Concerns over the potential impact of disinvestment have grown as national governments have become more active investors and as uncertainty over the risks associated with securities backed by sub-prime mortgages has increased volatility in financial markets. Actions taken by foreign investors to liquidate their holdings could affect the U.S. economy in a number of ways due to the role foreign investment plays in the United States and due to the current mix of economic policies the United States has chosen. The impact of any such action on the economy would also depend on the overall condition and performance of the economy and the financial markets. If the economy were experiencing a strong rate of economic growth, the impact of a foreign withdrawal likely would be minimal, especially given the dynamic nature of credit markets. If a withdrawal occurred when the economy were not experiencing robust rate of growth or if credit financial markets were under duress, the withdrawal could have a stronger effect on the economy.

The particular course of action foreign investors might choose to take and the overall strength and performance of the economy at the time of their actions could affect the economy in different ways. Congress likely would become involved as a result of its direct role in making economic policy and its oversight role over the Federal Reserve. In addition, the actions of foreign investors could complicate domestic economic policymaking. Foreign investors who decide to liquidate their holdings of one particular type of investment would normally need to look for other types of assets to acquire. While there are a multitude of possible strategies foreign investors could pursue, this analysis assesses the impact of four of the most likely strategies a single large foreign investor or a group of foreign investors could chooseto employ to reduce or withdraw entirely their holdings of U.S. financial assets:

A rapid liquidation of U.S. Treasury securities.

A shift in the make-up of foreign investors' portfolios among various dollar-denominated assets.

A rapid shift from dollar-denominated assets to assets denominated in other currencies.

A slow shift in the make-up of future accumulations of assets away from dollar-denominated assets to assets denominated in currencies other than the dollar.

This report will be updated as events warrant.

OVERVIEW

Foreign capital inflows are playing an important role in the economy. Such inflows bridge the gap between U.S. supplies and demands for credit, thereby allowing consumers and businesses to finance purchases at interest rates that are lower than they would be without overseas capital inflows. Similarly, capital inflows allow federal, state, and local governments to finance their budget deficits at rates that are lower then they would be otherwise. These foreign capital inflows allow the Nation to support expenditures exceeding its current output level and finance its trade deficit. A sharp reduction in those inflows likely would complicate domestic efforts at making and conducting economic policies.

To date, the world economy has benefitted from the stimulus provided by the nation's combination of fiscal and monetary policies and trade deficit. Foreign investors now hold slightly less than 50% of the publicly held and publicly traded U.S. Treasury securities, 25% of corporate bonds, and about 12% of U.S. corporate stocks.[66] The large foreign accumulation of U.S. securities has spurred some observers to argue that this foreign presence in U.S. financial markets increases the risk of a financial crisis, whether as a result of the uncoordinated actions of market participants or by a coordinated withdrawal from U.S. financial markets by foreign investors for economic or political reasons. Concerns are also growing that over the long run U.S. economic policies and the accompanying large deficit in its international trade accounts could have a negative impact on global economic developments, especially for the economically less developed countries.

Some observers are concerned that a foreign investor with significant holdings in the United States or a group of foreign investors could engage in an abrupt and large-scale liquidation of dollar-denominated securities, particularly a sell-off of U.S. Treasury securities. These observers argue that the vast sums of dollars held and managed by some foreign governments, termed sovereign wealth funds, raise the prospects of such a coordinated withdrawal, because the funds potentially increase the ability of foreign governments to instigate a rapid withdrawal. It is uncertain, though, what types of events could provoke a coordinated withdrawal from U.S. securities markets. Although unlikely, a coordinated withdrawal from U.S. financial markets potentially could be staged by foreign investors for economic or political reasons or it could arise from a sharp drop in U.S. equity prices as a result of an uncoordinated correction in market prices. Also, concerns over the ability of the federal government to service its foreign debt and a loss of confidence in the ability of national U.S. policy makers to conduct economic policies that are perceived abroad as prudent and stabilizing could spur some foreign investors to reassess their estimates of the risks involved in holding dollar-denominated assets. In other cases, international linkages that connect national capital markets could be the conduit through which events in one market are quickly spread to other markets and ignite an abrupt, seemingly uncoordinated, withdrawal of capital. Such concerns have increased as financial markets have attempted to re-price the perceived risks and uncertainty associated with securities backed by sub-prime mortgages.

A liquidation of capital could be limited to one segment of the credit markets as one foreign investor or a group of foreign investors attempted to adjust the composition of their portfolios. A withdrawal also could mark a major shift in investment strategies by foreign investors as they shifted away from dollardenominated securities. Short of a financial crisis, events that cause some foreign investors to adjust their portfolios likely would have short-run negative effects on U.S. interest rates and on the international exchange value of the dollar. However, should a large group of foreign investors make a permanent shift in their strategies to limit or to reduce their purchases of U.S. securities, such actions likely would complicate efforts to finance budget deficits. Given the current mix of economic policies, the loss of capital inflows would affect U.S. interest rates, domestic investment, and the long-term rate of growth of the economy. Such a loss of capital inflows would be especially troublesome if it occurred during a time when concerns over the rate of growth in the economy were increasing. During periods when the rate of economic growth is slowing, the Federal Reserve generally resorts to reducing interest rates to stimulate the economy. However, the loss of capital inflows would tend to push the Federal Reserve to raise interest rates to attract more capital inflows. Congress likely would find itself embroiled in any such economic or financial crisis through its direct role in conducting fiscal policy and in its indirect role in the conduct of monetary policy through its supervisory responsibility over the Federal Reserve.

Some observers are also concerned that recent developments in the financial system have increased the possibility of a financial crisis. They contend that such a crisis could damage the international financial system in the short run and could potentially affect the performance of individual economies. The rapid expansion of market activity through the consolidation of equity exchanges and the development of complex financial instruments and hybrid securities that are traded across national borders has spurred some analysts to question whether the market and financial innovations have outpaced the efforts of regulators. For instance, concerns about the risks of sub-prime mortgage-backed securities has eroded some investors' confidence in the underlying stability of some segments of the global financial system. As a result, some observers argue that improvements in the financial system that arise from greater market efficiencies by spreading risk across national borders may be blunted, because the underlying risks of certain widely traded financial instruments have become more difficult to assess. Consequently, some commentators maintain that the risks of a domestic financial crisis spreading across national borders have become more pervasive because of the rapid internationalization of financial services. Others note that by expanding into financial activities that were not part of the original core business of financial services, providers may be exposed to new and additional types of risk for which they are not well prepared. According to the IMF, "there is little empirical evidence to date to determine whether cross-border diversification of financial institutions reduces or increases firm-specific or systemic vulnerabilities."[67]

FOREIGN INVESTMENT IN THE U.S. ECONOMY

Capital flows are highly liquid, can respond abruptly to changes in economic and financial conditions, and exercise a primary influence on exchange rates and through those rates onto global flows of goods and services. As indicated in **Figure 1**, these capital inflows are composed of official inflows, primarily foreign governments' purchases of U.S. Treasury securities, and private inflows composed of portfolio investment, which includes foreigners' purchases of U.S. Treasury and corporate securities, financial liabilities, and direct investment in U.S. businesses and real estate. In 1996, total foreign capital inflows to the United States reached over $551 billion, but by 2000 foreign capital inflows totaled more than $1 trillion, as indicated in **Table 1**. Such inflows were reduced in 2001 and 2002 as the growth rate of the U.S. economy slowed, but grew to over $1.8 trillion in 2007 as the rate of economic growth improved. Private capital inflows comprise more than three-fourths of the total capital inflows, with foreign purchases of corporate securities, stocks and bonds being the main components of these inflows. In 2007, official inflows attributed to foreign governments accounted for 22% of total foreign capital inflows, down slightly from the share recorded in 2006.

Economists generally attribute the rise in foreign investment in the United States to comparatively favorable returns on investments relative to risk, a surplus of saving in other areas of the world, the well-developed U.S. financial system, and the overall stability of the U.S. economy. These net capital inflows (inflows net of outflows) bridge the gap in the United States between the amount of credit demanded and the domestic supply of funds, likely keeping U.S. interest rates below the level they would have reached without the foreign capital. These capital inflows also allow the United States to support expenditures exceeding its current output level and finance its trade deficit, because foreigners are willing to "lend" to the United States in the form of exchanging goods, represented by U.S. imports, for such U.S. assets as stocks, bonds, and U.S. Treasury securities. Such inflows, however, put upward pressure on the dollar, which tends to push up the price of U.S. exports relative to its imports and to reduce the overall level of exports. Furthermore, foreign investment in the U.S. economy drains off some of the income earned on the foreign-owned assets that otherwise would accrue to the U.S. economy as foreign investors repatriate their earnings back home.

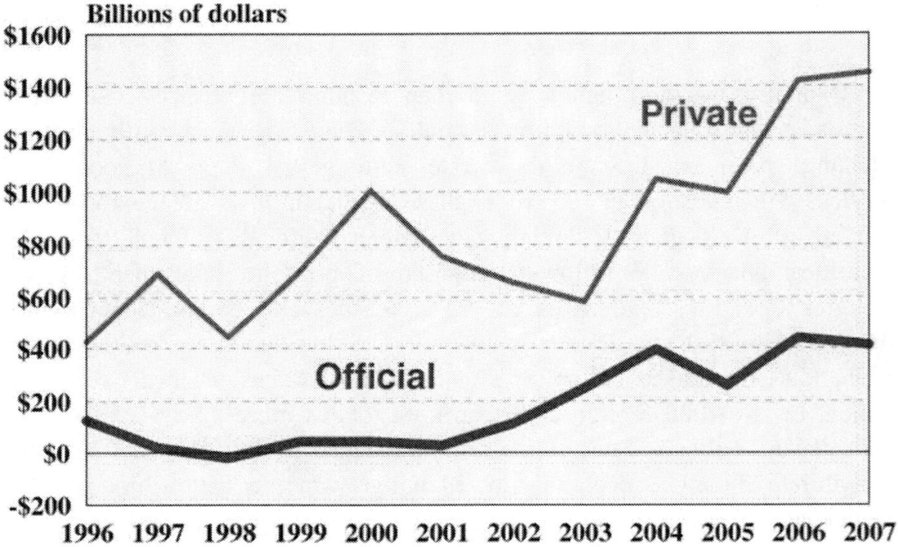

Source: Department of Commerce

Figure 1. Foreign Private and Official Capital Inflows Into the United States, 1996-2007

Flow of Funds in the U.S. Economy.

Figure 2 shows the net flow of funds in the U.S. economy. The flow of funds accounts measure financial flows across sectors of the economy, tracking funds as they move from those sectors that supply the capital through intermediaries to sectors that use the capital to acquire physical and financial assets.[68] The net flows show the overall financial position by sector, whether that sector is a net supplier or a net user of financial capital in the economy. Because the demand for funds in the economy as a whole must equal the supply of funds, a deficit in one sector must be offset by a surplus in another sector.

Table 1. Capital Inflows to the United States, 1996-2007 (in billions of dollars)

			Private assets					
Year	Total	Official assets	Total	Direct investment	Treasury securities	Corporate securities	U.S. currency	Other
1996	$551.1	$126.7	$424.4	$86.5	$147.0	$103.3	$17.4	$70.2
1997	706.8	19.0	687.8	105.6	130.4	161.4	24.8	265.5
1998	423.6	-19.9	443.5	179.0	28.6	156.3	16.6	62.9
1999	740.2	43.5	696.7	289.4	-44.5	298.8	22.4	130.5
2000	1,046.9	42.8	1,004.1	321.3	-70.0	459.9	5.3	287.6
2001	782.9	28.1	754.8	167.0	-14.4	393.9	23.8	184.5
2002	768.2	114.0	654.3	72.4	100.4	285.5	21.5	174.4
2003	829.2	248.6	580.6	39.9	113.4	251.0	16.6	159.7
2004	1,440.1	394.7	1,045.4	106.8	107.0	369.8	14.8	477.0
2005	1,204.2	259.3	995.0	109.0	132.3	450.4	19.0	234.3
2006	1,859.6	440.3	1,419.3	180.6	-35.9	592.0	12.6	670.2
2007	1,863.7	412.7	1,451.0	204.4	166.3	391.9	10.9	677.3

Source: Bach, Christopher L., U.S. International Transactions in 2007, *Survey of Current Business*, April 2008, p. 48.

[66] For more information, see CRS Report RL32964, *The United States as a Net Debtor Nation: Overview of the International Investment Position*, by James K. Jackson.

[67] *Op. cit., Global Financial Stability Report*, p. 107.

[68] Teplin, Albert M., the U.S. Flows of Funds Accounts and Their Uses, *Federal Reserve Bulletin*, July 2001, pp. 431-441.

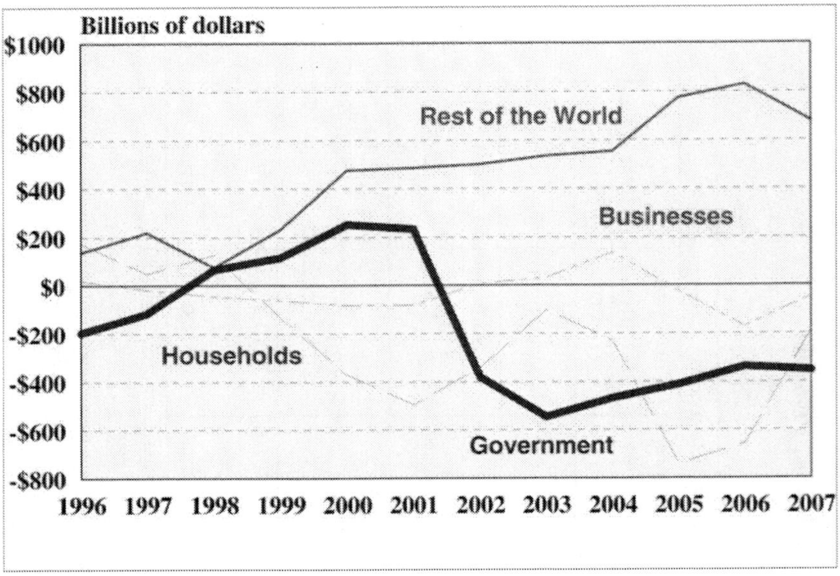

Source: Federal Reserve

Figure 2. Flows of Funds in the U.S. Economy, 1996-2007

Generally, the household sector, or individuals, provides funds to the economy, because individuals save part of their income, while the business sector uses those funds to invest in plant and equipment that, in turn, serve as the building blocks for the production of additional goods and services. The government sector (the combination of federal, state, and local governments) can be either a net supplier of funds or a net user, depending on whether the sector is running a surplus or a deficit, respectively. The interplay within the economy between saving and investment, or the supply and uses of funds, tends to affect domestic interest rates, which move to equate the demand and supply of funds. Shifts in the interest rate also tend to attract capital from abroad, denoted by the rest of the world (ROW) in **Table 2**.

As **Table 2** indicates, from 1996 through 1998, the household sector ran a net surplus, or provided net savings to the economy. The business sector also provided net surplus funds in 1996, or businesses earned more in profits than they invested. The government sector, primarily the federal government, experienced net deficits, which decreased until 1998, when the federal government and state and local governments experienced financial surpluses. Capital inflows from the rest of the world rose and fell during this period, depending on the combination of household saving, business sector saving and investment, and the extent of the deficit or surplus in the government sector.

Starting in 1999, the household sector began dissaving, as individuals spent more than they earned. Part of this dissaving was offset by the government sector, which experienced a surplus from 1998 to 2001. As a result of the large household dissaving, however, the economy as a whole experienced a gap between domestic saving and investment that was filled with large capital inflows. Those inflows were particularly large in nominal terms from 2000 to 2006, as household dissaving continued and as government sector surpluses turned to historically large deficits in nominal terms. Such inflows have kept interest rates below the level they would have reached without the inflows, but have put added pressure on the international exchange value of the dollar.

Table 2. Flow of Funds of the U.S. Economy, 1996-2007 (in billions of dollars)

Year	Households	Businesses	Government			ROW
			Total	State and Local	Federal	
1996	175.2	19.8	-196.8	-1.2	-195.6	137.9
1997	47.4	-18.3	-116.6	-47.5	-69.1	219.6
1998	128.0	-45.7	64.8	48.8	16.0	75.0
1999	-132.7	-62.6	115.3	9.9	105.4	231.7
2000	-371.0	-82.9	252.5	54.5	198.0	476.3
2001	-494.4	-82.9	233.4	35.4	198.0	485.4
2002	-343.4	8.7	-382.6	-95.6	-287.0	501.7
2003	-101.8	30.3	-546.3	-70.4	-475.9	535.4
2004	-230.6	136.8	-468.6	-32.9	-435.7	554.4
2005	-741.0	-26.1	-413.1	-16.1	-397.9	773.3
2006	-656.9	-170.5	-338.8	-50.3	-283.0	829.3
2007	-188.0	-45.4	-353.3	-90.7	-284.0	677.4
I 2007	6.4	-57.9	-486.5	-95.7	-387.8	728.1
II 2007	-1,199.6	10.8	-130.2	-64.3	-65.9	621.4
III 2007	618.5	-86.9	-435.9	-84.8	-351.1	441.9
IV 2007	-177.8	-47.6	-449.5	-118.2	-331.3	918.2
I 2008	219.2	-90.9	-636.8	-162.7	-474.1	592.1

Source: Board of Governors of the Federal Reserve System, *Flow of Funds Accounts of the United States, Flows and Outstandings First Quarter 2008*, June 5, 2008.

In 2007, capital inflows fell by about $150 billion from the amount recorded in 2006. This drop in capital inflows reflected a sharp drop in household dissaving, a decrease in business sector dissaving and an increase in the deficits experienced by State and Local governments. In the first quarter of 2008, the flow of funds show a large drop in capital inflows from the rest of the world, from $918 billion in the fourth quarter of 2007 through the first quarter of 2008. In addition, households turned from a dissaving of $178 billion in the fourth quarter of 2007 to a net saving of $219 billion in the first quarter of 2008, reflecting the growing concern among households over the state of the economy. The Federal Reserve has reported[1] that in the first quarter of 2008, households experienced a drop in their net worth of $1.7 trillion.

As the flow of funds data indicate, foreign capital inflows augment domestic U.S. sources of capital, which in turn keep U.S. interest rates lower than they would be without the foreign capital. Indeed, economists generally argue that it is this interplay between the demand for and the supply of credit in the economy that drives the broad inflows and outflows of capital. As U.S. demands for capital outstrip domestic sources of funds, domestic interest rates rise relative to those abroad, which tends to draw capital away from other countries to the United States.

Foreign and Domestic Sources of Funds

The United States also has benefitted from a surplus of saving over investment in many areas of the world that has provided a supply of funds and accommodated the overall shortfall of saving in the country. This surplus of saving has been available to the United States because foreigners have remained willing to loan that saving to the United States in the form of acquiring U.S. assets, which have accommodated the growing current account deficits. Over the past decade, the United States experienced a decline in its rate of saving and an increase in the rate of domestic investment. The large increase in the nation's current account deficit would not have been possible without the accommodating inflows of foreign capital.

Foreign capital inflows, while important, do not fully replace or compensate for a lack of domestic sources of capital. Capital mobility has increased sharply over the last 20 years, but economic analysis shows that a nation's rate of capital formation, or domestic investment, seems to be linked primarily to its domestic rate of saving. This phenomenon was first presented in a paper published in 1980 by Martin Feldstein and Charles Horioka.[2] The Feldstein-Horioka paper maintained that despite the dramatic growth in capital flows between nations, international capital mobility remains somewhat limited so that a nation's rate of domestic investment is linked to its domestic rate of saving.[3]

Foreign Capital and the Value of the Dollar

Liberalized capital flows and floating exchange rates have greatly expanded the amount of capital flows between countries. These capital transactions are undertaken in response to commercial incentives or political considerations that are independent of the overall balance of payments or of particular accounts. As a result of these transactions, national economies have become more closely linked, the process some refer to as "globalization." The data in **Table 3** provide selected indicators of the relative sizes of the various capital markets in various countries and regions and the relative importance of international foreign exchange markets. In 2006, these markets amounted to $500 trillion, or more than 30 times the size of the U.S. economy. Worldwide, foreign exchange and interest rate derivatives, which are the most widely used hedges against movements in currencies, were valued at $347 trillion in 2006, 78% larger than the combined total of all public and private bonds, equities, and bank assets. For the United States, such derivatives total nearly three times as much as all U.S. bonds, equities, and bank assets.

Another aspect of capital mobility and capital inflows is the impact such capital flows have on the international exchange value of the dollar. Demand for U.S. assets, such as financial securities, translates into demand for the dollar, because U.S. securities are denominated in dollars. As demand for the dollar rises or falls according to overall demand for dollar-denominated assets, the value of the dollar changes. These exchange rate changes, in turn, have secondary effects on the prices of U.S. and foreign goods, which tend to alter the U.S. trade balance. At times, foreign governments have moved aggressively in international capital markets to acquire the dollar directly or to acquire Treasury securities in order to strengthen the value of the dollar against particular currencies.

Table 3. Selected Indicators of the Size of the Global Capital Markets, 2006
(in billions of U.S. dollars)

	Gross Domestic Product (GDP)	Total Official Reserves	Bonds, Equities, and Bank Assets				Exchange Market Derivatives		
			Total	Stock Market Capitalization	Debt Securities	Bank Assets	Total	OTC Foreign Exchange Derivatives	OTC Interest Rate Derivatives
World	48,434.4	5,091.5	194,462.7	50,826.6	68,200.9	74,465.2	395,557.0	48,620.0	346,937.0
European Union	13,658.0	252.7	73,983.7	13,068.8	23,192.3	37,736.3	N.A.	N.A.	N.A.
Euro Area	10,586.1	157.5	54,822.0	8,419.1	18,761.1	26,719.2	145,903.0	18,280.0	127,623.0
United States	13,194.7	54.9	56,822.0	19,569.0	27,050.1	10,202.9	154,799.0	40,488.0	114,311.0
Japan	4,377.1	879.7	20,109.5	4,795.8	8,723.7	6,590.0	58,329.0	10,579.0	47,750.0

Source: *Global Financial Stability Report*, International Monetary Fund, April 2008, Statistical Appendix, Table 3.

Note: Total derivatives does not include equity and commodity-linked derivatives.

Also, the dollar is heavily traded in financial markets around the globe and, at times, plays the role of a global currency. Disruptions in this role have important implications for the United States and for the smooth functioning of the international financial system. This prominent role means that the exchange value of the dollar often acts as a mechanism for transmitting economic and political news and events across national borders. While such a role helps facilitate a broad range of international economic and financial activities, it also means that the dollar's exchange value can vary greatly on a daily or weekly basis as it is buffeted by international events.[4]

A triennial survey of the world's leading central banks conducted by the Bank for International Settlements in April 2007 indicates that the *daily* trading of foreign currencies through traditional foreign exchange markets[5] totals more than $3.2 trillion, up sharply from the $1.9 trillion reported in the previous survey conducted in 2004. In addition to the traditional foreign exchange market, the over-the-counter (OTC)[6] foreign exchange derivatives market reported that daily turnover of interest rate and non-traditional foreign exchange derivatives contracts reached $2.1 trillion in April 2007. The combined amount of $5.3 trillion for daily foreign exchange trading in the traditional and OTC markets is more than three times the *annual* amount of U.S. exports of goods and services. The data also indicate that 86.3% of the global foreign exchange turnover is in U.S. dollars, slightly lower than the 88.7% share reported in a similar survey conducted in 2004.[7]

In the U.S. foreign exchange market, the value of the dollar is followed closely by multinational firms, international banks, and investors who are attempting to offset some of the inherent risks involved with foreign exchange trading. On a daily basis, turnover in the U.S. foreign exchange market[8] averages $664 billion; similar transactions in the U.S. foreign exchange derivative markets[9] average $607 billion, nearly double the amount reported in a similar survey conducted in 2004.[10] Foreigners also buy and sell U.S. corporate bonds and stocks and U.S. Treasury securities. Foreigners now own slightly less than 50% of the total amount of outstanding U.S. Treasury securities that are publicly held and traded.[11]

WITHDRAWAL OF FOREIGN INVESTMENT

This section analyzes four possible strategies a single large foreign investor or a group of foreign investors could employ to reduce or withdraw entirely their holdings of financial assets in the United States. These strategies include

- a rapid liquidation of U.S. Treasury securities,
- a shift in the make-up of foreign investors' portfolios among various dollar-denominated assets,
- a rapid shift from dollar-denominated assets to assets denominated in other currencies, and
- a slow shift in the make-up of future accumulations of assets away from dollar-denominated assets to assets denominated in currencies other than the dollar.

Sudden Withdrawal from U.S. Treasury Securities

The large holdings of U.S. Treasury securities by foreign governments have led some observers to consider the prospect of a withdrawal from the U.S. Treasury securities market by a single foreign government. At the first hint that a foreign government was attempting to liquidate all or even a large part of its holdings of U.S. Treasury securities, the price of such Treasury securities likely would plummet in U.S. securities markets and the market rate of interest would rise, perhaps appreciably, in the first few hours or days. For instance, on November 7, 2007, a report, that was later repudiated, asserted that Chinese officials were considering shifting some of China's foreign currency reserves, reportedly worth $1.4 trillion, in dollars and in such dollar-denominated assets as Treasury securities, out of dollar-denominated securities. Acting on the report, investors sold securities and the dollar. As a result, the broad Dow Jones industrial average plunged 360 points in one day and the dollar sank against other major currencies.[12] In response to the fall in the exchange value of the dollar, indexes of equities markets in Europe and Japan also fell.

Such cross-border spill-over effects are not new, but potentially have become more pervasive as a result of the broad linkages that have been forged among the once-disparate national financial systems. As an example, concerns in U.S. capital markets in early June 2006 over prospects that a rise in consumer prices and in the core inflation rate would push the Federal Reserve to raise key U.S. interest rates sparked a drop in prices in U.S. capital and equity markets where inflation concerns quickly spread to markets in Europe and Asia as equity prices fell in those markets as well.[13]

If a foreign investor with large U.S. holdings or a group of foreign investors attempted to launch a withdrawal from U.S. Treasury securities, investors and other market participants would calculate quickly the expected effects of those intended actions on market prices, interest rates, and the exchange value of the dollar and would then act swiftly on those anticipated effects. As a result, the prices of Treasury securities likely would drop sharply, while interest rates would rise, because the price of such securities is inversely related to the interest rate. In addition, the dollar likely would fall in value relative to other currencies, because the shift away from dollardenominated assets would increase demand for and the prices of other currencies relative to the dollar. Consequently, the drop in the price of Treasury securities and the drop in the exchange value of the dollar would significantly discount the value of any Treasury securities that would be sold and sharply reduce the proceeds for any investor participating in such a sell-off. As a result, the potentially large financial losses that would attend an attempt to liquidate assets rapidly are likely to dissuade most investors from employing such a strategy.

The drop in the prices of Treasury securities and the decline in the exchange value of the dollar, however, probably would be short-lived. Foreign investors selling Treasury Securities presumably would do so in order to acquire non-dollardenominated assets. Such a shift in demand from U.S. Treasury securities to other foreign securities would drive up the prices of those securities and the exchange value of foreign currencies. As a result, the lower prices for Treasury securities and for the dollar would offer other investors arbitrage and investment opportunities to acquire assets that investors likely would deem to be temporarily undervalued. As a result, investors likely would move to acquire Treasury securities and the dollar, which means that demand would increase for both the low-priced Treasury securities and the lower-valued dollar, which would drive up the prices of both assets. Such a response could significantly blunt, or even entirely reverse, the initial drop in prices of the securities and of the dollar. Given the dynamic nature of finance and credit markets and the instantaneous communication of information, such actions likely would occur within a very short time frame.

For instance, fears spread rapidly after the terrorist attacks on New York and Washington on September 11, 2001, that foreigners would curtail their purchases of U.S. financial assets and reduce the total inflow of capital into the U.S. economy. Following the attacks, foreign governments and private investors did reduce their purchases of Treasury securities from pre-attack levels and the value of the dollar fell relative to other major currencies. These effects were fully reversed within 30 days, however, as currency traders forged a short-lived agreement not to profit from the attacks and the Federal Reserve undertook actions on its own and in concert with central bankers and financial ministers around the globe to ensure the smooth operation of the international financial markets.[14] Similarly, the Federal Reserve likely would not be expected to sit by idly while foreign investors attempted a coordinated withdrawal from U.S. equity markets, if those actions threatened to undermine the stability of the markets.

The overall performance of the U.S. economy at the time of any attempted withdrawal would also influence the economic effect of the withdrawal. For instance, if the U.S. economy were experiencing a robust rate of economic growth, the impact of a withdrawal by foreign investors likely would be minimal, both in the short run and in the long run. However, if such a withdrawal were to occur at a time when the U.S. economy were not experiencing a robust rate of economic growth, or if the U.S. credit and financial markets were under duress, such a withdrawal may well have a more pervasive effect by undermining investors' confidence in the stability and performance of the markets and could result in higher interest rates and a lower exchange value of the dollar over the short run and prolong the adjustment process. In addition, actions that change foreign investors' assessment of the underlying risks of the financial system or that undermine foreign investors' confidence in the stability of the financial system could prod some foreign investors to reassess the composition of their portfolios.

For instance, at the time of the rumored Chinese withdrawal from U.S. securities, U.S. financial markets already were strained by concerns over the impact of record oil prices and potentially large losses associated with sub-prime mortgaged-backed securities. As a result, the Dow Jones industrial average of U.S. stocks moved erratically through the end of November 2007. By the end of November 2007, the Dow was down nearly 290 points from where it had been following the loss of 360 points on November 7, 2007.

Diversify Portfolios among Dollar-Denominated Assets

Another possible course of action some foreign investors could pursue would be to diversify abruptly the composition of their portfolios by replacing a sizeable portion of their holdings of U.S. Treasury securities with other dollar-denominated assets. As foreign investors traded Treasury securities for other assets, the price of Treasury securities would decline and the prices of other assets would rise as demand shifted away from Treasury securities and toward other dollar-denominated assets. Because total demand for dollar-denominated assets would remain constant, there likely would be little movement in the exchange value of the dollar, but the shift of demand would alter the relative prices of various domestic assets. Such shifts in demand are not a rare occurrence, but happen frequently as investors change their evaluations of the relative value of corporate equities, corporate bonds, and Treasury securities and in response to changes in economic policies and actions by the Federal Reserve.

If foreign investors attempt to alter abruptly the composition of their portfolios away from Treasury securities, the prices of such securities would fall and the prices of corporate bonds and equities would rise, reflecting the shift in demand. If investors perceived this shift in demand and, therefore, the shift in prices, as a onetime adjustment in the composition of foreign investors' portfolios, some investors likely would take advantage of the rise in prices in equities and bonds to sell their holdings and take their profits at what likely would be perceived to be overvalued prices and, conversely, buy Treasury securities at what they would view as temporarily undervalued prices. After these adjustments, market prices likely wouldsettle at prices that would be close to or equal to those that had existed prior to the original shift in demand by foreign investors.

Shift Away from Dollar-Denominated Assets

Another course of action some foreign investors could pursue would be to pare down their holdings of dollar-denominated assets through a relatively swift liquidation of part of their holdings of dollar-denominated assets. In this case, a single foreign investor or a group of foreign investors would sell off part of their holdings of such dollar-denominated assets as corporate stocks and bonds or Treasury securities and possibly even direct investments (investments in U.S. businesses and real estate), although selling direct investments in this manner seems less likely given the generally long-run strategies investors use in acquiring them. If some foreign investors attempted to accomplish such a readjustment in their portfolios quickly by liquidating a portion of their holdings of corporate stocks and bonds and of Treasury securities, the prices of those assets would fall, given the current pervasive role foreign investors play in most U.S. financial markets.

In addition, because the foreign investors would be liquidating their dollar-denominated assets in order to acquire assets denominated in other currencies, the exchange value of the dollar would fall relative to the price of foreign currencies. The drop in the prices of dollar-denominated equities and bonds combined with the lower exchange value of the dollar would erode the expected profits of any investor selling such securities and likely would attract the interest of other foreign investors, who presumably could liquidate their now higher-priced foreign securities and leverage their now higher-valued foreign currency to acquire dollar-denominated assets. Furthermore, U.S. multinational firms may well take advantage of the highervalued foreign currency to repatriate part of the profits of their foreign affiliates, which would boost the balance sheet of their U.S. parent company, possibly even using the repatriated profits to acquire their own stock. Such repatriated profits likely would put upward pressure on the exchange value of the dollar, because foreign earnings would have to be converted into dollars before they were repatriated. Similarly, foreign firms operating in the United States likely would retain their profits rather than suffering a loss in value by translating those profits into higher priced foreign currencies in order to repatriate their profits back to their foreign parent company. Presumably, such profits could be used to augment investments within the United States.

Slow Shift Away from Dollar-Denominated Assets

Finally, some foreign investors could decide to shift away from dollar-denominated assets by engaging in a long-term shift in the rate at which they accumulate such assets. Such a strategy would have the benefit of avoiding the large short-run shifts in the prices of financial assets and in the exchange value of the dollar that would attend any attempt by a group of foreign investors to make a rapid adjustment in the composition of their portfolios. A decrease in the inflow of capital from abroad would reduce the domestic availability of capital and place upward pressure on credit and financial assets as interest rates would rise to equate the demand and supply of credit. For the U.S. economy as a whole, a long-term shift away from dollar-denominated assets by foreign investors could have a slightly negative impact on the economy over the long run given the current mix of economic policies. A reduction in the inflow of foreign investment would tend to push down the prices of stocks and bonds and push up interest rates since those wanting credit would be competing for a smaller pool of funds. The price of Treasury securities would fall as the Federal government would be required to raise interest rates in order to attract domestic and foreign investors to acquire Treasury securities, which would raise the cost of financing the Federal government's budget deficit.

In addition, the shift from dollar-denominated assets would tend to push up the exchange value of foreign currencies relative to that of the dollar because an increase in demand for foreign assets would also raise demand for foreign currencies. The lower-valued dollar would raise the price of U.S. imports, particularly of raw materials and manufactured goods, which would put upward pressure on consumer and wholesale prices and tend to affect most negatively those sectors of the economy that are especially sensitive to movements in interest rates: the housing and automobile sectors. The decline in the international exchange value of the dollar also would tend to favor those industries and sectors of the economy that export. As long as the international exchange value of the dollar remained relatively low compared with other currencies, the exported goods sectors of the economy likely would expand by attracting more capital and labor and the imported goods sector of the economy would decline, assuming that all other things in the economy remained constant.

CONCLUSIONS

It is not uncommon for investors to adjust the composition of their portfolios as economic and financial conditions change. Given the recent surge in foreign investors' accumulation of dollars and dollar-denominated assets, it is not unreasonable to expect that from time to time they will also attempt to adjust the composition of their portfolios between corporate stocks and bonds, U.S. Treasury securities, and direct investments in U.S. businesses and real estate. A long-term shift away from dollar-denominated assets, however, could have a negative effect on the long-term rate of investment, productively, and the rate of growth in the U.S. economy. Such a shift in the value of the dollar would tend over the long run to benefit the exported goods sector of the economy, but it could also complicate efforts to conduct domestic economic policies. Although there are numerous other currencies that might attract investors, the dollar continues to be the most widely traded currency around the globe, which means it likely will retain its desirability as an investment asset and as a medium of exchange for some time to come. Also, the vast and deep capital markets in the United States combined with the highly developed banking and legal systems continue to make investments in U.S. financial assets attractive to foreign investors, despite short-run changes in perceptions of risk or economic performance.

Should a foreign investor with large financial holdings in the United States or a group of investors attempt to liquidate abruptly their holdings of assets such as Treasury securities, they would experience a severe loss in the value of those assets first as they attempted to sell their large holds in the market and then as they attempted to convert their dollar holdings into other currencies. As a result of these losses, it seems unlikely that a foreign investor with large holdings or a group of foreign investors would attempt to liquidate their securities quickly. A more likely course of action would be for foreign investors to adjust the composition of their portfolios slowly over time.

If only one or a few foreign investors engaged in a strategy to liquidate part of their U.S. financial holdings, their actions alone are likely to have a limited impact on the economy over the short run, because market forces would be expected to adjust to attract other foreign investors to replace those who had withdrawn. However, if a broad range of foreign investors, for whatever reason, decided to reduce their holdings of dollar-denominated assets, interest rates in the United States likely would rise in response to market forces that would place them above the level where they would have been if the foreign capital inflows had remained at their higher levels. A higher level of interest rates would lead some firms to reduce their level of borrowing and investing and spur some households to curtail their consumption, especially of such interest sensitive products as housing and automobiles, which usually are financed over long periods of time. Over the long run, the lower level of investment by firms could be expected to result in a lower rate of growth in productivity and, therefore, in a lower rate of growth in the economy.

In addition, if foreign investors were to attempt an abrupt adjustment to the composition of their portfolios that disrupted the financial markets or the broader economy, the Federal Reserve would not be expected to stand idly by on the sidelines. In such circumstances, the Federal Reserve has shown some agility in intervening on its own to stabilize credit markets and to move in coordination with other central banks. On December 11, 2007, for instance, the Federal Reserve decreased the federal funds rate and the discount rate on loans between banks by a quarter of a percentage point to ease credit conditions. Then, on December 12, 2007, the Federal Reserve announced that it would make $40 billion and perhaps more available to commercial banks in short-term loans to ease domestic liquidity issues and another $24 billion available to European central banks that had become so concerned about potential losses from U.S. mortgage-backed securities that they had begun to hoard cash and were unwilling to make loans to each other except at unusually high interest rate premiums.[15] Such willingness on the part of the Federal Reserve to intervene in the financial markets to ensure stability likely makes a prolonged financial crisis arising from a liquidation of financial assets by one foreign investor or a group of foreign investors unlikely, even if those investors are foreign governments.

ENDNOTES

[1] Board of Governors of the Federal Reserve System, *Flow of Funds Accounts of the United States, Flows and Outstandings, First Quarter 2008*, June 5, 2008.

[2] Feldstein, Martin, and Charles Horioka, Domestic Saving and International Capital Flows, *The Economic Journal*, June, 1980, pp. 314-329; Feldstein, Martin, *Aspects of Global Economic Integration: Outlook for the Future*. NBER Working Paper 7899, September 2000, pp. 9-12.

[3] Developments in capital markets have improved capital mobility since the Feldstein-Horioka paper was published and have led some economists to question Feldstein and Horioka's conclusion concerning the lack of perfect capital mobility. (Ghosh, Atish R., International Capital Mobility Amongst the Major Industrialized Countries: Too Little or Too Much?, *The Economic Journal*, January 1995, pp. 107-128.) Indeed, some argue that short-term capital flows among the major developed economies are highly liquid, perhaps too liquid, and seem to be driven as much by short-term economic events and speculation as they are by longer term economic trends.

[4] Samuelson, Robert J., "Dangers in a Dollar on the Edge," *The Washington Post*, December 8, 2006, p. A39.

[5] Traditional foreign exchange markets are organized exchanges which trade primarily in foreign exchange futures and options contracts where the terms and condition of the contracts are standardized.

[6] The over-the-counter foreign exchange derivatives market is an informal market consisting of dealers who custom-tailor agreements to meet the specific needs regarding maturity, payments intervals, or other terms that allow the contracts to meet specific requirements for risk.

[7] *Triennial Central Bank Survey: Foreign Exchange and Derivatives Market Activity in 2007*. Bank for International Settlement, September 2007, pp. 1-2. A copy of the report is available at [http://www.bis.org/publ/rpfx07.pdf].

[8] Defined as foreign exchange transactions in the spot and forward exchange markets and foreign exchange swaps. A spot transaction is defined as a single transaction involving the exchange of two currencies at a rate agreed upon on the date of the contract; a foreign exch ange swap is a multi-part transaction that involves the exchange of two currencies on a specified date at a rate agreed upon at the time of the conclusion of the contract and then a reverse exchange of the same two currencies at a date further in the future at a rate generally different from the rate applied to the first transaction.

[9] Defined as transactions in foreign reserve accounts, interest rate swaps, cross currency interest rate swaps, and foreign exchange and interest rate options. A currency swap commits two

counterparties to exchange streams of interest payments in different currencies for an agreed upon period of time and usually to exchange principal amounts in different currencies as a pre-agreed exchange rate; a currency option conveys the right to buy or sell a currency with another currency as a specified rate during a specified period.

[10] *The Foreign Exchange and Interest Rate Derivatives Markets: Turnover in the United States April 2007*. The Federal Reserve Bank of New York, April, 2004. pp. 1-2. A copy of the report is available at [http://www.newyorkfed.org/markets/triennial/fx_survey.pdf].

[11] *Treasury Bulletin*, March 2007, Table OFS-2, p. 48.

[12] Grynbaum, Michael M., and Peter S. Goodman, Markets and Dollar Sink as Slowdown Worry Increases. *The New York Times*, November 8, 2007.

[13] Masters, Brooke A., Pondering the Bear Necessities, *The Washington Post*, June 7, 2006, p. D1; Samuelson, Robert J., Global Capital On the Run, *The Washington Post*, June 14, 2006, p. A23.

[14] For more information, see CRS Report RS21102, *International Capital Flows Following the September 11 Attacks*, by James K. Jackson.

[15] Federal Reserve Press Release, December 12, 2007; Irwin, Neal, "Fed to Team With Central Banks on Credit," *The Washington Post*, December 12, 2007; Norris, Floyd, and Vikas Bajaj, "Fed Joins Other Banks to add Cash," *The New York Times*, December 12, 2007.

In: Foreign Investment In U.S. Securities
Editors: Declan J. Byrne
ISBN: 978-1-60876-084-8

Chapter 5

THE UNITED STATES AS A NET DEBTOR NATION: OVERVIEW OF THE INTERNATIONAL INVESTMENT POSITION

James K. Jackson

SUMMARY

The international investment position of the United States is an annual measure of the assets Americans own abroad and the assets foreigners own in the United States. The net position, or the difference between the two, sometimes is referred to as a measure of U.S. international indebtedness. Although this designation is not strictly correct, the net international investment position does reveal the difference between the total assets Americans own abroad and total amount of assets foreigners own in the United States. These assets generate flows of capital into and out of the economy that have important implications for the value of the dollar in international exchange markets. Some Members of Congress and some in the public have expressed concerns about the U.S. net international investment position because of the role foreign investors are playing in U.S. capital markets and the potential for large outflows of income and services payments. Some observers also argue that the U.S. reliance on foreign capital inflows leaves the economy vulnerable to financial crises. This report will be updated as events warrant.

BACKGROUND

The U.S. international investment position represents the accumulated value of U.S.-owned assets abroad and foreign-owned assets in the United States measured on an annual basis at the end of the calendar year. Some observers refer to the net of this investment position (or the difference between the value of U.S.-owned assets abroad and the value of foreign-owned assets in the United States) as a debt, or indicate that the United States is in a net debtor position, because the value of foreign-owned assets in the United States is greater than the value of U.S.-owned assets abroad. In fact, the nation's international investment position is not a measure of the nation's indebtedness similar to the debt borrowed by some developing countries, but it is an accounting of assets. By year-end 2007, the latest year for which data are available, the overseas assets of U.S. residents totaled approximately $17 trillion, while foreigners had acquired about $20 trillion in assets in the United States, with direct investment measured at historical cost. As a result, the U.S. net international investment position was about $2.6 trillion in the negative with direct investment measured at historical cost, as indicated in **Table 1**.

Table 1. U.S. Net International Investment Position (in billions of dollars)

Type of Investment	2004	2005	2006	2007
Net international investment position of the United States:				
With direct investment at current cost	-2,245.4	-1,925.1	-2,225.8	-2,441.8
With direct investment at market value	-2,355.8	-1,850.9	-1,849.3	-1,727.5
With direct investment at historical cost	-2,470.7	-2,129.9	-2,399.4	-2,653.6
Financial derivatives		57.9	59.8	83.5
U.S.-owned assets abroad:				
With direct investment at current cost	9,340.6	11,961.6	14,381.3	17,640.0
With direct investment at market value	10,204.6	12,947.8	15,900.0	19,455.1
With direct investment at historical cost	8,893.3	11,445.3	13,900.0	17,098.4
Financial derivatives		1,190.0	1,239.0	2,284.6

Table 1. (Continued)

Type of Investment	2004	2005	2006	2007
U.S. official reserve assets	189.6	188.0	219.9	277.2
U.S. Government assets, other	83.1	77.5	72.2	94.5
U.S. private assets:				
With direct investment at current cost	9,068.0	10,506.0	12,850.3	14,983.7
With direct investment at market value	9,932.3	11,492.2	14,368.9	16,798.8
With direct investment at historical cost	8,620.7	9,989.7	12,369.0	14,442.1
Direct investment abroad:				
— At current cost	2,498.5	2,651.7	2,936.0	3,332.8
— At market value	3,362.8	3,638.0	4,454.6	5,148.0
— At historical cost	2,051.2	2,135.5	2,454.7	2,791.3
Foreign securities	3,545.4	4,329.3	5,604.5	6,648.7
Bonds	985.0	1,011.6	1,275.5	1,478.1
Corporate stocks	2,560.4	3,317.7	4,329.0	5,170.6
U.S. claims by US nonbanking concerns	793.6	1,018.5	1,163.1	1,176.0
U.S. claims reported by US banks	2,230.5	2,506.5	3,146.7	3,826.2
Foreign-owned assets in the United States:				
With direct investment at current cost	11,586.1	13,886.7	16,607.1	20,081.8
With direct investment at market value	12,560.7	14,798.7	17,749.2	21,182.6
With direct investment at historical cost	11,364.1	13,575.2	16,299.4	19,752.0
Financial derivatives		1,132.1	1,179.2	2,201.1
Foreign official assets in the United States	2,011.9	2,306.3	2,825.6	3,357.0
Foreign private assets:				
Type of Investment	**2004**	**2005**	**2006**	**2007**
With direct investment at current cost	9,574.2	10,448.3	12,602.3	14,543.7

Table 1. (Continued)

Type of Investment	2004	2005	2006	2007
With direct investment at market value	10,548.8	11,360.3	13,744.4	15,644.5
With direct investment at historical cost	9,352.2	10,136.8	12,294.6	14,214.0
Direct investment in the United States:				
— At current cost	1,742.7	1,906.0	2,151.6	2,422.8
— At market value	2,717.4	2,818.0	3,293.7	3,523.6
— At historical cost	1,520.7	1,594.5	1,843.9	2,093.0
U.S. Treasury securities	561.6	643.8	567.9	734.8
U.S. other securities	3,995.5	4,353.0	5,372.4	6,132.4
— Corporate and other bonds	2,035.1	2,243.1	2,824.9	3,299.3
— Corporate stocks	1,960.3	2,109.9	2,547.5	2,833.1
U.S. currency	272.0	280.4	282.6	272.0
U.S. liabilities by U.S. nonbanking concerns	600.2	658.2	797.5	959.5
U.S. liabilities reported by U.S. banks	2,402.2	2,606.9	3,430.3	4,022.2

Source: Nguyen, Elena L., The International Investment Position of the United States at Yearend 2007, *Survey of Current Business*, July 2008. p. 9.

Foreign investors who acquire U.S. assets do so at their own risk and accept the returns accordingly, unlike the debt owed by developing countries where debt service payments are guaranteed in advance. The returns on the assets in the investment position, except for bonds, are not guaranteed and foreign investors gain or lose on them in the same way as U.S. domestic investors. As Table 1 indicates, these investments include such financial assets as corporate stocks and bonds, government securities, and direct investment[1] in businesses and real estate. The value of these assets, measured on an annual basis, can change as a result of purchases and sales of new or existing assets; changes in the financial value of the assets that arise through appreciation, depreciation, or inflation; changes in the market values of stocks and bonds; or changes in the value of currencies. The Department of Commerce also uses three different methods for valuing direct investments that yield roughly comparable estimates for the net position, although the three methods do provide estimates on U.S. direct investment abroad and foreign direct investment that can be considerably different at times.

VALUING INVESTMENTS

The Department of Commerce provides updated estimates on the nation's international investment position each year, typically in July, based on data for the previous year through the end of the calendar year. Except for direct investment, all of the accounts in the international investment position are estimated directly by the Department of Commerce's Bureau of Economic Analysis (BEA) relative to readily observable market prices. For example, the value of positions in portfolio investments (securities), gold, loans, currencies, and bank deposits can be directly estimated by the BEA based on the face values or market prices of recent transactions.

Estimating the value of direct investments, however, presents a number of challenges. According to the Department of Commerce, these challenges arise because foreign direct investments, "typically represent illiquid ownership interests in companies that may possess many unique attributes — such as customer base, management, and ownership of intangible assets — whose values in the current period are difficult to determine, because there is no widely accepted standard for revaluing company financial statements at historical cost into prices of the current period."[2]

As a result, the Department of Commerce estimates the U.S. international investment position in three ways, reflecting three different accounting methods for estimating the value of direct investments: historical cost; current cost; and market value. Initially, direct investments are valued at historical cost, or the cost at the time of the investment. This historical cost value can become outdated because it is not updated to account for changes in the value of an investment through appreciation, or through internal growth and expansion, or through changes in various intangible assets. The current cost approach estimates the value of capital equipment and land at their current replacement cost using general cost indexes, and inventories, using estimates of their replacement cost, rather than at their historical cost. The third measure, market value, uses indexes of stock market prices to revalue the owners' equity share of direct investment.

For the most part, the current cost and historical cost estimates have tracked closely together for U.S. direct investment abroad and for foreign direct investment in the United States, as indicated in **Figures 1 and 2**, respectively. These two measures of direct investment demonstrate a steady increase in the value of the investments over the 26-year period from 1982 to 2007. The market value estimate of direct investment, however, displays a markedly different pattern. These estimates spiked during the rapid runup in stock market values in the 1990s and then dropped sharply when market values declined at the end of the 1990s. The market value estimates rose sharply again in 2003 through 2007, as the rebound in stock market values pushed up the estimated market value of firms. As a result, the market value of U.S. direct investment abroad was estimated at $5.1 trillion in 2007, pushing the overall U.S. position to $19.5 trillion, compared with an estimate of the historical cost of $2.8 trillion for foreign direct investment in the United States and an overall position of $17.1 trillion and $3.3 trillion for current cost direct investment position and $15.4 trillion position for current cost estimate. Since the early 1980s, the annual value of foreign direct investment in the United States has been greater at times than the annual value of U.S. direct investment abroad, but the accumulated value of U.S. direct investment abroad, or the position, has continuously been valued higher.

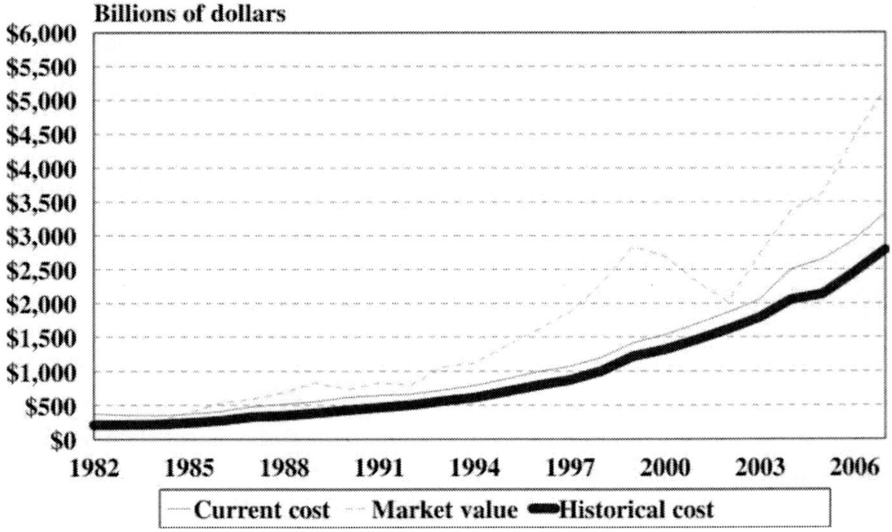

Source: Department of Commerce

Figure 1. U.S. Direct Investment Abroad: Estimated Value of Accumulated Position, 1982-2007

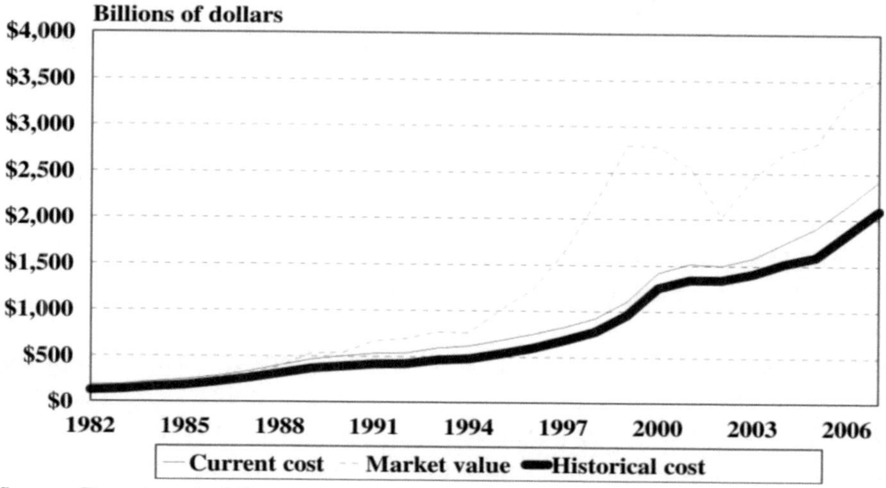

Source: Department of Commerce

Figure 2. Foreign Direct Investment in the United States: Estimated Value of Accumulated Position, 1982-2007

INVESTMENT PATTERNS

Foreign direct investment in U.S. businesses surged in the mid-1980s and has at times outpaced the annual amount of U.S. direct investment abroad. For various reasons, U.S. direct investment abroad and foreign direct investment in the United States have tended to track together so that the annual flows increase or decrease somewhat in tandem,[3] except in 2005, when U.S. direct investment abroad dropped sharply as U.S. parent firms reduced the amount of reinvested earnings going to their foreign affiliates for distribution to the U.S. parent firms in order to take advantage of one-time tax provisions in the American Jobs Creation Act of 2004 (P.L. 108- 357). Between 2001 and 2006, U.S. direct investment outflows have been greater than similar inflows. As a whole, however, foreign investment among all U.S. assets has been greater than U. S. investment abroad, which has tended to push the net U.S. international investment position further into a negative position. This is not the first time in the nation's history that the U.S. net international investment position has been negative.

Early in the nation's history as the United States made the transition from being a developing economy to being a major economic superpower, foreign investment flowed into capital development projects such as railroad and canal construction which aided the westward expansion and the development of heavy industries. By 1920, foreigners had withdrawn many of their assets from the United States to finance World War I, which turned the United States into a net creditor. This net creditor position grew unabated after World War II and into the 1980s, when large inflows of foreign investment once again turned the nation into a net international investment debtor.

The U.S. net debtor status continued to grow through the 1990s and into the 2000s, as indicated by **Figure 3**. By year-end 2007, U.S. assets abroad are estimated to have reached $17.1 trillion, while foreign owned assets in the United States reached $19.8 trillion. As a result, the U.S. net international investment position was estimated at a negative $2.8 trillion, or equivalent to about 19% of U.S. Gross Domestic Product, marking a substantial increase in the relative size of the net investment debt position over the previous decade, as indicated in **Table 2.** The net investment position worsened by over $250 billion during 2007, with direct investment measured at historical cost. According to the two other measures for direct investment — current cost and market value — the net investment position was valued at about negative $2.4 trillion and $1.7 trillion, respectively.

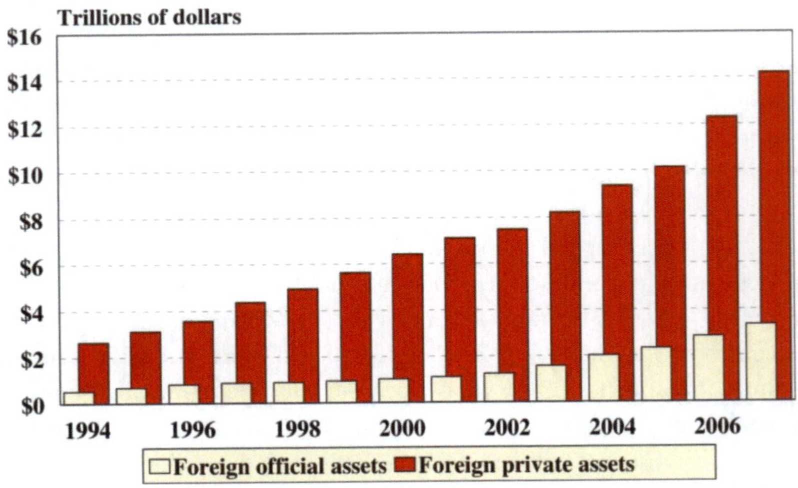

Source: Department of Commerce

Figure 3. Foreign Official and Private Investment Positions in the United States, 1994-2007

Table 2. U.S. International Investment Status (billions of dollars)

	U.S.-Owned Assets Abroad	Foreign-Owned Assets in the United States	U.S. Net International Investment Position	U.S. Gross Domestic Product	Relative Share of U.S. Gross Domestic Product
1980	929.8	569.0	360.8	5,161.7	7%
1985	1,287.4	1,233.1	54.3	6,053.7	1%
1990	2,179.0	2,424.3	-245.3	7,112.5	3%
1991	2,286.5	2,595.7	-309.3	7,100.5	4%
1992	2,331.7	2,762.9	-431.2	7,336.6	6%
1993	2,753.6	3,060.6	-307.0	7,532.7	4%
1994	2,987.1	3,310.5	-323.4	7,835.5	4%
1995	3,486.3	3,944.7	-458.5	8,031.7	6%
1996	4,032.3	4,527.4	-495.1	8,328.9	6%
1997	4,567.9	5,388.6	-820.7	8,703.5	9%
1998	5,090.9	5,990.9	-900.0	9,066.9	10%
1999	5,965.1	6,740.6	-775.5	9,470.3	8%
2000	6,023.4	7,455.8	-1,432.4	9,817.0	15%
2001	6,075.9	8,053.6	-1,977.7	9,890.7	20%
2002	6,401.8	8,585.0	-2,183.2	10,074.8	22%
2003	7,380.9	9,613.7	-2,132.8	10,960.8	20%
2004	8,893.3	11,364.1	-2,470.7	11,685.9	21%
2005	11,445.3	13,575.2	-2,130.0	12,433.9	17%
2006	13,900.0	16,299.4	-2,399.4	13,194.7	18%
2007	17,098.4	19,752.0	-2,653.6	13,841.3	19%

Source: Department of Commerce

The foreign investment position in the United States continues to increase as foreigners acquire additional U.S. assets and as the value of existing assets appreciates. These assets are broadly divided into official and private investments reflecting transactions by governments among themselves and transactions among the public. At times, some observers have been concerned about the amount of foreign official investment in the U.S. economy, particularly in U.S. Treasury securities and, more recently, purchases of U.S. businesses by foreign governments. As **Figure 4** indicates, official asset holdings were valued at about $3.3 trillion in 2007, or about 16% of the total foreign investment position, a share that has remained relatively stable over the 15-year period of 1993 through 2007. Official assets include such monetary reserve assets as gold, the reserve position with the International Monetary Fund (IMF), and holdings of foreign currency. An important component of foreign official holdings in the United States is the acquisitions of U.S. Treasury securities by foreign governments. At times, such acquisitions are used by foreign governments, either through coordinated actions or by themselves, to affect the foreign exchange price of the dollar. Foreign currency holdings account for a relatively small share of the total foreign investment position.

Private asset holdings are comprised primarily of direct investment in businesses and real estate, purchases of publicly traded government securities, and corporate stocks and bonds. As indicated in **Figure 5**, the composition of U.S. assets abroad and foreign-owned assets in the United States is different in a number of ways. The strength and uniqueness of the U.S. Treasury securities markets make these assets sought after by both official and private foreign investors, whereas U.S. investors hold few foreign government securities. As a result, foreign official assets in the United States far outweigh U.S. official assets abroad. Both foreign private and official investors have been drawn at times to U.S. government securities as a safe haven investment during troubled or unsettled economic conditions.

Of all the accounts, inward and outward direct investments are the most closely matched, demonstrating the appeal of such investments to both U.S. and foreign investors. In fact, the United States is unique in that it not only is the largest foreign direct investor in the world, but it is also the largest recipient of direct investment in the world. Foreign investors also have been attracted to U.S. corporate stocks and bonds for the same reasons domestic U.S. investors have invested in them.[4] The decline in the overall value of U.S. corporate stocks after 2000, however, curbed the rate of growth of foreign purchases of these assets. A similar decline in the value of foreign stocks and the depreciation in the value of the U.S. dollar relative to a broad range of currencies reduced the dollar value of American-owned stock holdings abroad. Claims by private banks are also included in the international investment accounts and represent a broad range of international financial transactions, including financing for short-term trade credits associated with exports and imports of merchandise goods.

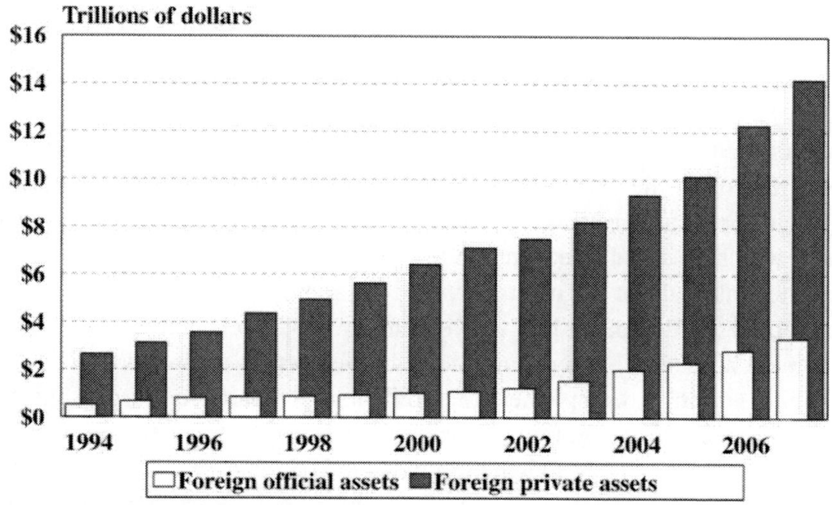

Source: Department of Commerce

Figure 4. Foreign Official and Private Investment Positions in the United States, 1994-2007

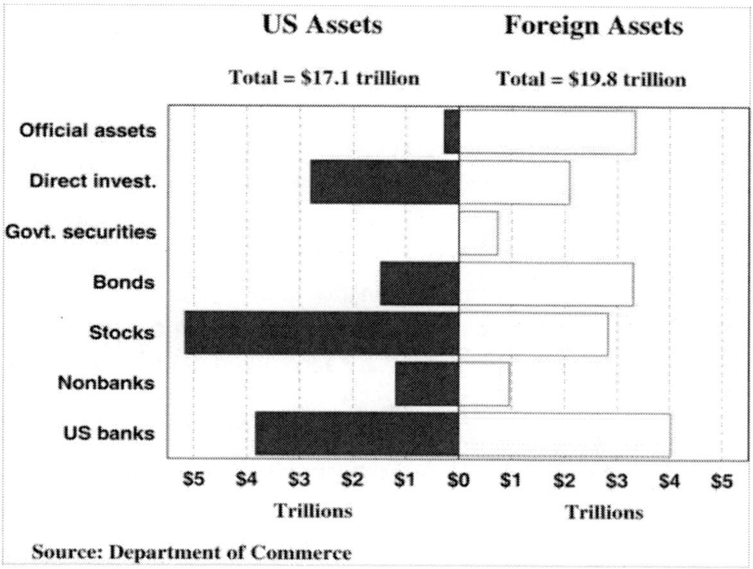

Source: Department of Commerce

Figure 5. U.S. and Foreign Investment Position, By Major Component, 2007

International Investment: Sources and Economic Impact

International investment not only has an impact on the U.S. economy, but it is affected by the economy. For U.S. investors, foreign markets provide them with opportunities to seek out the greatest returns for their investments, returns which are repatriated back to the United States. In addition, U.S. direct investment abroad, for the most part, tends to stimulate U.S. exports, which in turn stimulates the most productive sectors of the economy.[5] U.S. direct investment abroad is highly sought after by developing countries which want the capital not only to supplement their own limited domestic sources, but they also want American technology and expertise.

Foreign capital inflows augment domestic U.S. sources of capital, which, in turn, keep U.S. interest rates lower than they would be without the foreign capital. Indeed economists generally argue that it is this interplay between the demand for and the supply of credit in the economy that drives the broad inflows and outflows of capital. As U.S. demands for capital outstrip domestic sources of funds, domestic interest rates rise relative to those abroad, which tends to draw capital away from other countries to the United States.

The United States also has benefitted from a surplus of saving over investment in many areas of the world that has provided a supply of funds. This surplus of saving has been available to the United States because foreigners have remained willing to loan that saving to the United States in the form of acquiring U.S. assets, which have accommodated the growing current account deficits. Over the past decade, the United States experienced a decline in its rate of savings and an increase in the rate of domestic investment, as indicated in **Table 3**. The large increase in the Nation's current account deficit would not have been possible without the accommodating inflows of foreign capital.

As **Table 3** indicates, compared with the 1994-2001 period, U.S. saving in 2007 declined by 3.4% of gross domestic product (GDP), while investment increased by 0.8% of GDP. This shift toward greater investment relative to saving was accommodated by an increase worldwide in saving relative to investment. Among other advanced economies and the newly industrialized economies in Asia, both saving and investment declined in 2007 relative to the 1994-2001 period, but investment declined more as a share of GDP than did saving, so in relative terms saving increased as a share of GDP. In the emerging developing economies, the developing economies of Asia (which includes China), and the Middle East, saving as a share of GDP increased faster, and in some cases much faster, than did investment, which also increased in most of these areas. The large inflows of foreign capital to the United States likely arise from the relatively more robust economic growth that occurred in the United States compared with almost any other area, the well-developed U.S. financial system, and the overall stability of the U.S. economy.

Table 3. Saving and Investment in Selected Countries and Areas; 1994-2001 and 2007 (Percentage of Gross Domestic Product)

Area/Country	Average, 1994-2001	2007	Change
World			
Saving	22.1	23.7	1.6
Investment	22.4	23.3	0.9
United States			
Saving	17.0	13.6	-3.4
Investment	19.6	18.8	-0.8
Other Advanced Economies			
Saving	21.6	20.0	-1.6
Investment	21.8	21.1	-0.7
Eurozone			
Saving	21.3	21.8	0.5
Investment	21.0	22.2	1.2
Japan			
Saving	29.3	28.6	-0.7
Investment	26.9	23.8	-3.1
Newly Industrialized Asian Economies			
Saving	33.0	32.0	-1.0
Investment	29.9	25.7	-4.2
Emerging Developing Economies			
Saving	24.1	33.0	8.9
Investment	24.8	28.8	4.0
Developing Asia			
Saving	32.7	44.7	12.0
Investment	32.4	37.9	5.5
Middle East			
Saving	25.2	44.7	19.5
Investment	22.1	24.9	2.8

Source: *World Economic Outlook*, International Monetary Fund, April 2008. p. 268-271.

Capital inflows also allow the United States to finance its trade deficit because foreigners are willing to lend to the United States in the form of exchanging the sale of goods, represented by U.S. imports, for such U.S. assets as stocks, bonds, and U.S. Treasury securities. Such inflows, however, put upward pressure on the dollar, which tends to push up the price of U.S. exports relative to its imports and reduce the overall level of exports. Furthermore, foreign investment in the U.S. economy drains off some of the income earned on the foreign-owned assets that otherwise would accrue to the U.S. economy as foreign investors repatriate their earnings back home.

Some observers are particularly concerned about the long-term impact of the U.S. position as a net international investment debtor on the pattern of U.S. international income receipts and payments. In 2007, the United States received $900 billion in income receipts (including receipts on royalties) on its investments abroad and paid out $761 billion in income payments (including payments on royalties) on foreign-owned assets in the United States for a net surplus of $139 billion in income receipts.[6] This surplus has varied over time as rising interest rates increases payments to foreign investors on such assets as Treasury securities and corporate bonds.[7] As the annual amount of foreign investment in the U.S. economy continues to exceed the amount of U.S. investment abroad, it seems inevitable that U.S. payments on foreign-owned assets will exceed U.S. receipts. A net outflow of income payments would act as a drag on the national economy as U.S. national income is reduced by the net amount of funds that are channeled abroad to foreign investors.

One of the positive areas of the income accounts is the income receipts the United States receives on U.S. direct investments abroad. Although the historical cost value of U.S. direct investment abroad and foreign direct investment in the U.S. are roughly equal, the United States earned $234 billion more on its direct investment assets abroad in 2007 than foreigners earned on their direct investments in this country, as indicated in **Figure 6**. As indicated previously, in 2005 U.S. parent firms reduced the amount of reinvested earnings going to their foreign affiliates for distribution to the U.S. parent firms in order to take advantage of one-time tax provisions in the American Jobs Creation Act of 2004 (P.L. 108-357). The Department of Commerce has analyzed data on direct investment to determine the source of the low rate of return of foreign direct investment relative to U.S. direct nvestment abroad.[8] This analysis concluded that the gap in the rate of return between U.S.-owned enterprises abroad and foreign-owned enterprises in the United tates is narrowing over time and seems to be related to the age of the investment, or that as foreigners' investments mature the rate of return of the assets approaches that of U.S. direct investment abroad.

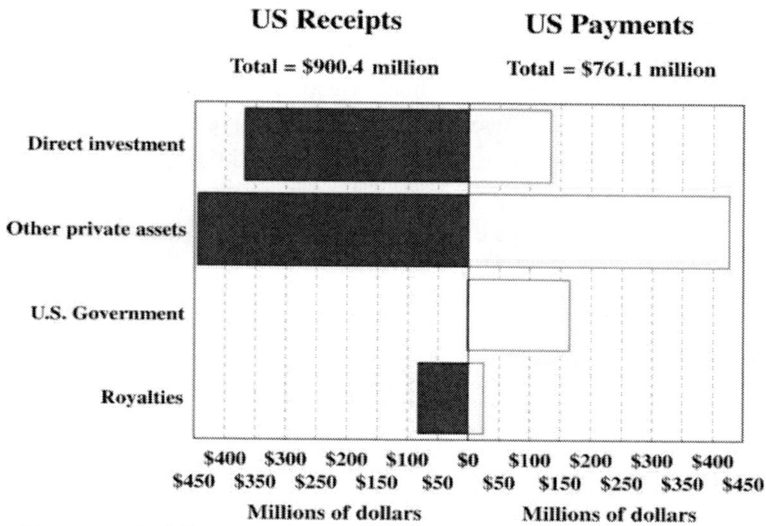

Source: Department of Commerce

Figure 6. U.S. Income Receipts and Payments on U.S.-Owned Assets Abroad and on Foreign-Owned Assets in the United States, 2007

The U.S. net surplus of income receipts arising from direct investments was offset to a large extent by large net income payments to foreign holders of U.S. government securities, which grew by 22% to $165 billion in 2007, up from the $135 billion it received in 2006. The overall U.S. income surplus was increased further by the income payments made to U.S. holders of foreign corporate stocks and bonds. The United States received $444 billion in income from the corporate stocks and bonds Americans owned abroad and paid out over $427 billion to foreign holders of U.S. corporate securities, for a net inflow of $17.8 billion in income receipts on such assets. In addition, the United States received $82 billion in royalties in 2007 on various products and on U.S.-licensed production technology, patents, and copyrighted material. This was more than double the $25 billion the United States paid foreigners in royalties on their investments in the United States.

Some observers also are concerned about the extensive amount of foreign investment overall in the U.S. economy and in U.S. financial assets. According to the estimates provided in **Table 4**, foreigners own approximately 20% of total U.S. wealth. Although foreign investors own a little less than 6% of total

U.S. fixed private capital stock, they own substantially larger shares of U.S. financial assets. For instance, foreign investors now own nearly 50% of total U.S. Federal debt and more than half of the outstanding publicly traded U.S. Treasury securities.[9] Some observers argue that such investments could spur an economic crisis in this country should foreign investors decide to pull their money out of the investments, whether for economic or political reasons. This possibility seems remote, however, given the negative impact such an action might have on the foreign investors themselves, but the concerns remain.[10]

Table 4. Estimates of Wealth in the United States, 2006 Current-Cost, Gross Stock Values (billions of dollars, percent)

Item	Total	Foreign Owned	Foreign Share
Fixed Private Capital	$31,816.50	$1,789.09	5.6%
Nonresidential	$14,715.00	$1,789.09	12.2%
— Agriculture, Forestry, and Fisheries	$542.80	$2.53	0.5%
— Mining	$1,158.80	$55.48	4.8%
— Construction	$238.70	$10.30	4.3%
— Manufacturing	$2,036.60	$593.61	29.1%
— Transportation	$984.70	$24.72	2.5%
— Wholesale Trade	$469.10	$252.03	53.7%
— Retail Trade	$936.50	$32.90	3.5%
— Finance, Insurance, Real Estate	$1,499.80	$291.27	19.4%
— Services	$3,559.10	$209.09	5.9%
Residential	$17,444.90		
— Farms	$98.30		
— Real Estate	$17,005.20		
Fixed Government Capital	$8,738.50		
— Equipment	$856.60		
— Structures	$7,881.90		
Consumer Durable Goods	$3,875.10		
Financial Assets	$35,576.92	$9,901.20	27.8%
— Federal Debt, Publicly Held	$4,924.72	$2,115.01	42.9%
— Corporate Stocks	$20,905.90	$2,538.72	12.1%
— Corporate Bonds	$9,746.30	$2,689.82	27.6%
— Other	$2,557.65		
Total	$80,009.02	$16,294.62	20.4%

Source: Nguyen, Elena L., The International Investment Position of the United States at Yearend 2006, *Survey of Current Business*, July 2007. p. 18-19; Wasshausen, David B., Fixed Assets and Consumer Durable Goods for 1997-2006, *Survey of Current Business*, September 2007. p. 21-32; Foreign Direct Investment in the United States, Detail for Historical-Cost Position and Related Capital and Income Flows, 2004-2006. *Survey of Current Business*, September 2007. Table 17; *Flow of Funds Accounts of the United States Flows and Outstandings, Second Quarter 2007*, September 17, 2007. Tables L212 and L213; *Treasury Bulletin*, Department of the Treasury, September 2007. Table FD-1.

CONGRESSIONAL RESPONSE

Despite expressing concerns at times about the U.S. net international investment position, Members of Congress generally have been reluctant to intervene in the investment process, whether inward or outward. Indeed, successive Congresses and Administrations have led international efforts to eliminate or reduce restraints on the international flow of capital. If the U.S. net investment position continues to turn more negative, prospects increase that the positive U.S. net income receipts will turn negative as U.S. income payments overwhelm U.S. income receipts. In such a case, the U.S. economy will experience a net economic drain as income that could be used to finance new U.S. businesses and investments will be sent abroad to satisfy foreign creditors. Such a drain likely will be small at first relative to the overall size of the economy, but it could grow rapidly if the economy continues to import large amounts of foreign capital.

Some observers are also concerned about the growing role foreign investment is playing in the economy by bridging the gap between domestic sources and demands for credit. One chief consideration is how the capital is being used. Investment funds that are flowing into direct investment and into corporate stocks and bonds presumably are being used to bolster investments in plant and equipment and other investments that aid in corporate productivity over the long run. As such, those investments may well provide a boost to U.S. economic growth well into the future. Foreign investment in U.S. Treasury securities directly aid in financing the Federal government's budget deficits and indirectly ease the Federal government's demands on domestic credit markets, which assists U.S. firms and consumer consumption by freeing up capital in the economy and by relieving some of the pressure on domestic interest rates.

One growing concern among some policymakers is the rising amount of investment by foreign governments in U.S. businesses, real estate, and portfolio assets (corporate stocks and bonds, and U.S. Government securities). Such investments by foreign governments are bolstered by the growing holdings of U.S. currency by foreign governments, known as sovereign wealth funds, which are estimated to amount to more than $2.5 trillion.[11] U.S. policy toward foreign investment generally has been one of acceptance and openness. Investments by foreign governments, however, are viewed by some as a new and different kind of investment that bears greater scrutiny. Such investments by foreign governments are viewed by some as contrary to longstanding U.S.

policies which have encouraged foreign governments to shift away from owning businesses enterprises and to support private ownership. For some observers, investments by foreign governments also raise the potential for official interference into a broad range of market activities. There is no evidence to date that ownership of various U.S. assets by foreign governments, by itself, has affected the management of those assets or the markets in which they exist in ways that differ from ownership by private foreign entities. Nevertheless, such concerns likely helped motivate Congress to pass, and President Bush to sign on July 26, 2007 **P.L. 110-49**, the Foreign Investment and National Security Act of 2007, which increases congressional oversight over acquisitions of U.S. businesses by foreign governments.

Some observers contend that a sharp decline in capital inflows or a sudden withdrawal of foreign capital from the economy could spark a financial crisis. Congress likely would find itself embroiled in any such financial crisis through its direct role in conducting fiscal policy and in its indirect role in the conduct of monetary policy through its supervisory responsibility over the Federal Reserve. Such a coordinated withdrawal seems highly unlikely, particularly since the vast majority of the investors are private entities that presumably would find it difficult to coordinate a withdrawal. Short of a financial crisis, events that cause foreign investors to curtail or limit their purchases of U.S. securities likely would complicate efforts to finance budget deficits in the current environment without such foreign actions having an impact on U.S. interest rates, domestic investment, and long-term rate of growth.

ENDNOTES

[1] The United States defines foreign direct investment as the ownership or control, directly or indirectly, by one foreign person (individual, branch, partnership, association, government, etc.) of 10% or more of the voting securities of an incorporated U.S. business enterprise or an equivalent interest in an unincorporated U.S. business enterprise. 15 CFR § 806.15 (a)(1). Similarly, the United States defines direct investment abroad as the ownership or control, directly or indirectly, by one person (individual, branch, partnership, association, government, etc.) of 10% or more of the voting securities of an incorporated business enterprise or an equivalent interest in an unincorporated business enterprise. 15 CFR § 806.15 (a)(1).

[2] Nguyen, Elena L., "The International Investment Position of the United States at Yearend 2007," *Survey of Current Business*, July 2008. p. 9.

[3] See CRS Report RL32461, *Outsourcing and Insourcing Jobs in the U.S. Economy: Evidence Based on Foreign Investment Data*, by James K. Jackson.

[4] For additional information, see CRS Report RL32462, *Foreign Investment in U.S. Securities*, by James K. Jackson.

[5] For additional information, see CRS Report RL32461, *Outsourcing and Insourcing Jobs in the U.S. Economy: Evidence Based on Foreign Investment Data*, by James K. Jackson.

[6] Sauers, Renee M., and Kristy L. Howell, U.S. International Transactions: First Quarter of 2008. *Survey of Current Business*, July 2008. P. 58.

[7] Whitehouse, Mark, U.S. Foreign Debt Shows Its Teeth AS Rates Climb. *The Wall Street Journal*, September 25, 2006. P. A1.

[8] Mataloni, Raymond, Jr., "An Examination of the Low Rates of Return of Foreign-Owned U.S. Companies," *Survey of Current Business*, March 2000, p. 55-73; and Landefeld, J. Steven, Ann M. Lawson, and Douglas B. Weinberg, "Rates of Return on Direct Investment," *Survey of Current Business*, August 1992, p. 79-86.

[9] For additional information, see CRS Report RL32462, *Foreign Investment in U.S. Securities*, by James K. Jackson.

[10] For a longer presentation of this topic, see CRS Report RL34319, *Foreign Ownership of U.S. Financial Assets: Implications of a Withdrawal*, by James K. Jackson.

[11] Weisman, Steven R., A Fear of Foreign Investments. *The New York Times*, August 21, 2007.

Chapter Sources

The following chapters have been previously published:

Chapter 1 – This is an edited, reformatted and augmented version of a Congressional Research Service publication, Report Order Code RL34314, dated March 5, 2009.

Chapter 2 - These remarks were delivered as testimony of Brad Setser Senior Economist, Roubini Global Economics and Research Associate, Global Economic Governance Programme, University College, Oxford Before the House Budget Committee, dated June 26, 2007.

Chapter 3 - This is an edited, reformatted and augmented version of a Congressional Research Service publication, Report Order Code RL32462, dated March 13, 2009.

Chapter 4 - This is an edited, reformatted and augmented version of a Congressional Research Service publication, Report Order Code RL34319, dated July 14, 2008.

Chapter 5 - This is an edited, reformatted and augmented version of a Congressional Research Service publication, Report Order Code RL32964, dated July 22, 2008.

INDEX

C

D

E

F

G

H

I

J

L

M

N